ONE WITH THE CREOSOTE
Memories of a Desert Child

ONE WITH THE CREOSOTE
Memories of a Desert Child

By Chris Tiffany

ONE WITH THE CREOSOTE
Memories of a Desert Child

FIRST EDITION
Copyright © 2020 by Chris Tiffany

All rights reserved. No part of this book may be used or reproduced in any manner whatsoever without written permission from the author, except in the case of brief quotations embodied in critical articles or reviews. For information, please address the author:
Chris Tiffany, P.O. Box 576, Solvang, CA 93464

International Standard Book Number 978-0-578-66625-9

Printed in the United States of America

Published by:
Desert Spirit Press
P.O. Box 87
Twentynine Palms, CA 92277

Book design & layout: Vickie Waite
Cover image: Creosote photograph by Chris Tiffany
Back cover: Photograph of the author by Lloyd Tiffany

Dedication

To my father, Joe Spangenberg, whose unexpected death in 1990 spawned these writings, in acknowledgement of the loving sacrifices he continually made for his family.

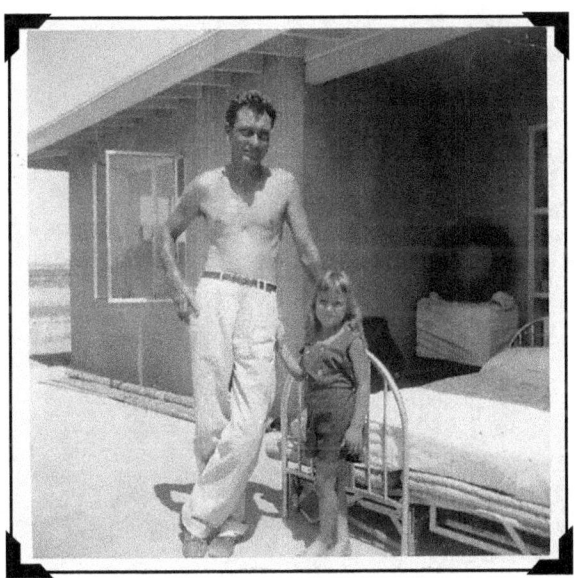

Joe Spangenberg and daughter Chris in 29 Palms, 1954.

Contents

	Page
Preface—"In Gratitude"	vi
Foreword: "Pilgrimage"	x
Growing Up Desert	1
Light and Shadow	41
Earth Musings	77
Circles of Reverie	101
Afterword: "The Unfinished Fence"	141
"In Memoriam"	145

Preface
"In Gratitude"

Without the unwavering loyalty of my sister, Patsy Keppner Walker, I would have no true audience for these accumulated memories. We have shared so much. How to thank her for believing in me so heart-fully?

My gratitude to Dorothy Jardin, my writing workshop guide, for empowering my journalistic style with expression through guided imagery, allowing the poetry of soul to emerge.

To Connie Rohde, my dear companion in work and play, I thank you for your confidence in me. You have a profound sense of recognizing hidden talent in others and encouraging them to bloom.

To my children, Pat and Kate, I love you. You prove daily what life's grandest blessings can be. To your father, Tim Carson, for guiding us to become who we are.

And without Lloyd (Murphy) Tiffany coming into my life, I would never, in my adulthood, have reentered my beloved desert so fully. Nor would I have come to know the community of special folks within this desertscape whom we befriended together. He has shown me the way, my forever moon-man. There are truly no words to express how much he means to me.

"The desert gets you, of course, old timers say, and there seems to be no better way to express it...You never know when it happens, or at what moment it first takes place, but the silence and majesty of the great spaces become a part of you, and the desert forges chains about your heart nothing on earth can break."

—Elizabeth Crozier Campbell
"The Desert Was Home"

Foreword

"Pilgrimage"
April 14, 1993

It is the quiet.
It is the sharp blue,
contrasting with the edges of the mountain ridges;
the pinkish tinted rocks,
the rustle of the breezes in the scrub brush,
the intensity of light.
It is the solitude and the colors that draw me here,
and the familiarity of scents—creosote bush, yucca and
mesquite.
It is the silence and the sounds.
Chirping bird calls and a distant passing car
you can hear for prolonged droning minutes.

The wisp of white crescent moon,
its round edge crisp yet soft against a periwinkle blue sky.
The shadows.
A 360-degree panorama of living desert.
Jumping cactus sparkling in the sunshine,
a blooming carpet of miniature yellow and lilac flowers,
the trail of a kangaroo rat's tail traced in the sand.
A tortoise hole.
Joshua trees crowned with pale yellow-green, rattle-shaped
blossoms.
The earth alive with a circular sea of black ants,
busily mounding soil and gathered plant particles
to form their sloping hill-home.

The call of a quail beckons me to come further. I venture deeper into the desert, following the twisting sandy wash criss-crossed with the tracks of tiny paws and birds' claws, creatures that have gone before me. I pinch the greasy tight leaves of the creosote bush between my fingers and breathe in the scents of my childhood.

My heart is so full! I breathe in the familiarity of it all—the sky, the dry morning breeze softly separating the strands of my sun-bleached hair, the intense noise of the silence. I soak it all up, into every cell of memory.

Later in the morning, as I pull into the parking lot at the entrance to Barker Dam in Hidden Valley, a crowd of boisterous school children shatters my reverie. Fortunately, for me, they are boarding their bus and the trail is quiet once again.

With the abundant winter rains, the lake's shoreline greets me sooner than expected, the water a tobacco brown when viewed up close, but a rippling blue in the distance, framed by a cirrus cloud-scattered sky, the new spring leaves of the willows, and the beige-peach-pink of the rocks.

Even with the background voices of other hikers, the serenity, depth of field and timelessness of the geology continue to overwhelm my senses.

A pair of grebes, male and female, floats silently past into the shadows of the rocks. An aquamarine dragonfly flits atop the water like a prehistoric helicopter, its wings shirring in the silence, which is suddenly interrupted by the honking of two coots in conversation. Bees buzz in the bushes behind me.

Again, I breathe it all in, perched on my rock at water's edge. Every crevice seems to harbor foliage in bloom. The juniper trees are trimmed in an abundant array of pale blue, hard round berries. The scent fills my head with nostalgia, bringing to mind the first Sauerbraten supper I prepared as a newlywed. I had picked those same berries in my very own yard to flavor the brine. I savor the memory.

The sun has gotten higher now. It's time to leave. On my way back to the car, the only sound is the scrunch of my shoes in the decomposed granite sand. A plump black lizard catches my eye as he gestures to me with his "push-ups" greeting. I greet him back, pumping with my hand in a similar motion. He stops and watches me, tilting his head in response to my body language before disappearing into the shade. I take one last, long look at Mount San Jacinto and San Gorgonio, their snowy peaks rising above the boulder-strewn horizon to the west.

The desert is a holy place to me.
I say the word with reverence.
And I realize that when I tell people,
"I'm from the desert,"
the words hold far more meaning
than they can possibly ascertain.

    I want to share the pure joy of this moment with those closest to me, to bring them here to fill them up with the beauty I feel. To help them understand the powerful hold the desert has on me.
    But this is my pilgrimage. I belong here. And I'm here, at this moment, for me.

Growing Up Desert

Early Imagery

The small faded turquoise duplex sits on a dirt alleyway off of Adobe Road, the town's main drag. My earliest memories of this place, our new home in the desert, are sunny ones. Sunlight streaming through the windows onto a lemony yellow shaggy throw rug on my mother's bedroom floor. Mom is folding laundry, stacks of neatly folded T-shirts and fluffy sweet smelling towels forming tidy sculptures on the bed. Her hands smooth out the wrinkles in quick, sure motions. It is a memory of serenity and safety.

It is 1953.

My older sister Patsy, eight years old, is a frail, thin boney-legged filly, whose continuous battle with asthma has thrust us from our oceanside home in San Pedro into a new life in Twentynine Palms. Like many other homesteaders who have settled in this remote desert town in the high desert of California, my parents are seeking an environment where their daughter can breathe instead of wheeze, where she can run and play and grow healthy in the dry desert air.

I am crazy about Patsy and am totally devoted to her. I have spent the first four years of my life sitting on her bed, making dollhouses and forts in the mounds of her quilts, drawing, reading comic books and watching Howdy Doody Time, being constantly at her side as she wheezed her way through early childhood.

We have left those playgrounds behind us. We are desert children now....

Dad had to stay behind in San Pedro that first year in Twentynine Palms. Work was scarce out here in the sticks. The Marine Corps Base, which now sprawls like a giant, self-sustaining city to the north, had served as an Air Training Station for gliders during World War II, but in 1953, the Marine Base, which later was to bring a whole new group of job-seeking emigrants to this desert outpost, was still in the planning stages.

As an adult reflecting back, I'm sure that this first year in the duplex, alone in an isolated town with two young children, was a long and lonely one for my mother, but now it is an eye-blinking blur of indistinct memories....

A wild wind whirls the dust into the skies. The sand stings the skin and whips away anything not battened down across the wide-open desert fields. The ashen tan sky is alive. We sit and listen to the whistling winds and mimic the hissing sound that pushes its way through the gaps in the windows, like air forced through clenched teeth with lips held in a tight oval "woooo."

When the roaring stops and the singing sands cease to blow, we rush outside and discover that our little tin bowl of tadpoles has blown away. Frantically we search, Mom's nightgown wrapping around her legs in the subsiding windstorm, as she helps us look for the lost critters. Sam, the produce man who comes out once a week in a big truck filled with tomatoes, giant watermelons, grapefruits and freshly harvested greens, joins in our search. We find the grey enamel bowl, but the water babies are gone. Lost in the restless sands. Sam pulls back the canvas tarp at the back of his truck and eases our loss with a gift of cantaloupe and ripe red cherries.

We have no car and, in fact, Mom does not know how to drive. Some time later Dad gets her a big old tan Hudson, in which she lurches up and down the sandy alleyways until she has mastered driving. But for now, having no car is not a problem. From the duplex we can walk everywhere, and we do.

We walk way up Adobe Road to the indoor sit-down movie theatre housed in a big old Quonset hut, and, most often, to the post office up in the Plaza. P.O. Box 305. My address. I tiptoe through the back door, a prowler peeking into the glass slots in the silver-grey boxes. Like little apartments they hold people's lives and all their stories. Large manila envelopes curled tightly with important papers inside. Thin fragile blue envelopes with colorful foreign stamps and the words Mit

Luftpost stenciled in blue printing. Letters from far-away places. Magazines. And pink hand-written cards that tell you to pick up a package! Peering through an empty box I can see the postmaster in grey slacks, his back to me, sorting piles of mail and whistling to himself, unaware of the pair of green eyes that watch him.

The library is on the way to the market. We check out three books each, books that take us to worlds far beyond our own. Mom reads the poetry of Madeleine's adventures, "In an old house in Paris that is covered with vines, lived twelve little girls in two straight lines." Or at bedtime she recites The Song of Hiawatha. "By the shores of Gitcheee Gumee, By the shining Big Sea Water, Stood the wigwam of Nokomis, Daughter of the Moon, Nokomis." The harmonious world of Indians, their sacred oneness with the sky, the owls, the pines, and the lilies of the prairies is revealed to us in the singsong tone of Mom's voice.

At the Desert Market Basket, Matt the butcher greets us with his warm dark eyes and jovial hello's. He cuts the chops exactly to Mom's liking. I put my face against the cool glass of the meat case and look at all the red and pink pieces of meat in their tidy rows. The market's aisles are cool and dark compared to the glare outside. Patsy and I put our hands into the icy cold water in the cooler and fish for bottles of Coca Cola, Nehi soda or Hire's Root Beer. Grape popsicles, chocolate-banana ice cream bars, or cups of vanilla ice cream with toppings of dark purple boysenberry lure us to the deep freeze. The walk to the market is a favorite outing.

A stinkbug crawls along in the sand. He is a loner. I tower above him and watch as he moves across the stones, wending his way through the dried grasses, moving his smooth black tank of a beetle body from side to side on bow-legged, bent spindly legs. Cootie legs.
When I poke at him with a stick, he stops and juts his torpedo rear end into the air, poised in a position that seems ideal for relief of heartburn or hemorrhoids! He releases a pungent rotten potato smell to fend me off. "Goodbye, Stink

Bugger. I'll leave you alone," I say, as I trot on up the wash on my own sun-bronzed, bent-kneed, spindly legs.

    I get the measles in the duplex. Lying on my cot in the living room, the intensity of the sunlight turns the heavy curtains at the western window into a wall of dark red flames. Hot. I close my aching eyes to escape the red-black heat, but it creeps behind my eyelids, burning and burning.

    The heat of the fever envelopes me in a tide of wild dreams. Spiders crawl on the ceiling, over my pillow. Black hairy spiders parading in an endless slow crawl, down the walls, out of the cracks in the plaster.

    Mom covers my face with a cold damp washrag to ease the torment. The cool darkness erases the curtain of flames at the window. I feel very small and far away. The voices in the kitchen are distant murmurs, familiar but incomprehensible. The rhythm of the language rocks me in a cradle of peaceful sleep...

Childhood Playgrounds, Lifetime Imprint

I am the mesquite, the jumping cactus,
the bare feet on massive granite boulders.
I am the buzzard nesting in oasis palm trees,
the huge white lizard with gentle, wise eyes,
with brown zigzag patterns on a scaly torso.
I am the tortoise, slow, solid and sure.
I am, after all these years,
a desert child with sunburned nose,
who holds in my heart
an ingrained love of light, shadow and the subtleties of color,
with a passion for open space
and the beauty of virgin native landscape.

A brand new stucco house on the corner of Cottonwood and Mara. *Rancho Marjo.* Margot and Joe's place. A full wall of wooden paned picture windows in the living room with a cement patio facing south. Two small bedrooms with metal-framed windows that crank open wide to let in the cool early morning breezes, powder blue tiled bath. Only a few neighborhood houses to the east and north. Two blocks from the sanctuary of Blessed Sacrament Church and a short walk through vacant fields to the Oasis of Mara, the northernmost oasis in the world. Our new playground.

You choose a neighborhood and you form a lifetime. Memories, philosophy of life, a way of being and perceiving the world, all are shaped by that singular choice.

Surrounded by acres and acres of open desert landscape and free to roam at will, without the confines of fences or sidewalks that dictate where to walk and play, free from the security consciousness and the protective barriers of urban living, we Spangenberg children, Patsy, Christy, Mark, Carl and Guy, are to grow up truly free, on Cottonwood Drive, in the bosom of the Mojave Desert.

The words ecology and environmental awareness are not part of our childhood vocabulary. Being bonded to the earth is simply a way of life for us as children of the desert.

As adults, we will, each and all, return often, to become one with the creosote, in Mark's words. To say hello and goodbye to the past, from which we have formed a lifetime. To the desert. The source of who we are...

We are two little girls. Sisters walking through the desert, exploring. One tall, long-limbed and freckled, brown hair pulled into a tight ponytail, bangs framing her face. The other shorter, with long blonde hair that blows freely in the breeze. Both barefooted and tanned with sleeveless blouses tied in a knot under our chests, midriffs bared. Shorts with elastic waistbands.

Our dogs, Misty and Lizzie, are with us. They are alert, their tails wagging happily as they trot beside us, unleashed and free. A jackrabbit bounds out of the bushes to our right. Suddenly we are hunters!

"Get it!" we yell to our dogs, pointing and running wildly. The dogs lower their bodies into a run and lunge after the prey. Our hearts are pounding. We shriek with excitement, our eyes following the hopping, bounding antics of the rabbit, who makes a wide circle, now far in the distance. Leaping over bushes, we run and run, arms pumping.

The dogs let out a yip in their own excited pursuit. Tails extended tensely, they stop, circling and sniffing the sand.

"We've lost him! Good chase!" We stoop to give Lizzie and Misty a praising pat. Our faces and arms are damp with sweat. Smiles in our squinted eyes, we walk side by side in the sunshine, two little girls, barefoot in a desert playground.

A solitary mesquite tree grows on the corner where the roads intersect in front of the Oasis. This is our fortress, our private ship, our tree house.

We climb into the dry branches with their scratchy, slivered rust-brown bark and sit in our concealed perches, which we have made by nailing boards into the tree's rough limbs. There we play for hours in the bright desert sunshine, unaware of any worlds other than our own.

Nestled between the hairy roots of the mesquite deep in the sand are bandaid boxes filled with our secret buried treasures. We line the sand with battalions of army men, tanks and fighter planes, scraping foxholes to hide in and mounding the earth into bunkers. Passionate rock fights ensue.

Slabs of juicy red watermelon become naval warships, the tough black sailor seeds tossing the enemy white seeds into the sea below.

In the shade of the mesquite brush we play "architect," building houses from balanced rocks, using brittle sticks for fencing and corrals, and small flat colorful stones pressed firmly into the sand for patios. From the entryways to anthills we gather handfuls of the coarse yellow grasses collected by the ants and spread it around our homes for lawns. We line our curving driveways with the yellow flowering sticky greasewood bush, with its springtime ornaments of white round compact pollen balls.

From our mesquite tree roost we look down at the little neighborhood we have built, admiring our plastic aquamarine Thunderbirds and red Corvettes, prizes retrieved from cereal boxes, parked securely in our popsicle stick carports.

Michael, Patsy and Tommy Pavelka, our next-door neighbors and constant playmates, come running breathlessly across the desert. "Come on!" they gasp. "We've found something over by the road!"

We launch ourselves out of our mesquite rocket ship and race across the fields, jumping over the scrub of grey-green cattle spinach brush, our tough bare feet skimming across the sand, our ankles yellow with the powder of wildflower pollen.

On a mound of sand lies a dead dog, a boxer. His bloated body has been dragged away from the side of the road and through the bushes on a piece of ragged burlap.

For a long time we just sit and stare at the carcass. Flies buzz around the dog and the hot afternoon breezes waft the decaying scent of carrion into our sun-freckled noses.

Suddenly the boys pick up rocks and throw them at the dog. The rocks ricochet off the tightly extended flesh of the animal's belly. We feel simultaneously sickened and silly. Caught up in the moment, we all toss stones at the carcass.

As quickly as the rock throwing started, it stops. We turn away from the animal and quietly walk away.

The following afternoon we return to see the progress of decay. Coyotes have dragged the body further into the desert, down the wash. Buzzards have taken turns at the dog's flesh. As the hot summer days dissolve the remains into the desert sands, we turn our attentions to other discoveries.

The pale yellow wildflowers look wan.
Singularly they cast a puny color,
but their masses wait for us
in delicate, breezy, silent song.
And when our legs and feet dash against them,
they cling to our bareness,
riding along with us on our adventures.
Dusting the hair on our legs, our bare feet, our ankles
with a talcum powder of pale flocked yellow.

Eager to go with us, the pollen dust clings.
We never brush it off.
It is our warrior paint,
our silk stockings,
our palomino forelegs.
Lying in wait on the sand, hunters,
the pollen dust coats our sweaty cheeks.

The wild yellow flowers,
with tough hairy roots
and pale grey-green incidental leaves.
Petals too numerous to count.
Too tiny to be seen singularly.
No-name flowers.
Common to our playing fields.
A dandelion blur of soft lemon yellow in the sand.

The pale, bleached-out yellow blossoms
are insignificant to us.
Until they dust our limbs with pollen power.

"Let's play horses!"

Transformed, we are wild Mustangs. I am a dark, short-coupled bay with black knees and a long ebony mane and tail. Patsy is a palomino with a sleek golden hide and champagne-colored flowing mane and tail. We pull our teeth back from our lips, giving each other a friendly horse laugh. Then, whinnying a challenge to a rival stallion, we stamp the dusty earth with our sharp hooves, tossing our long manes and snorting defiantly. Face to face, we rear up on our hind legs, pawing the air fiercely with nostrils flared and eyes wide. We round up our harem of mares, galloping wildly up the sandy wash, until, winded, we fall to the ground, our bodies lathered, foam at our mouths.

We can be man and horse at once.

I ride a bucking, untamed Appaloosa, a frisky horse wearing polka dotted pajamas. In the house, on Patsy's shoulders. Through the hallway, into the back bedroom, under the icy blasts of the swamp cooler. Wham! She is too tall. I catch my forehead on the doorjamb. Down I fall from my steed, clutching my skull on the corral floor of the living room. The life of a bronc buster is like that.

"Let's play horses!"

We drag rusty metal garbage barrels into the flat field across the street and ride our imaginary horses in fast figure eight's. Round and round the barrels we race in an intense gymkhana competition. We swat our hips with our flattened hands, pounding harder and tighter at full speed around the barrels.

Then we stand side by side and dash in a sprint to an assigned row of bushes and pull up in a hard slide, tightening up our reins and clicking commands to back up our horses. Later we stand, stretching out our legs and holding our necks straight and proud for a confirmation check by the judge.

Tossing a lasso over Mark's and Carl's tanned, wiry torsos as they circle the corral that we have lined out in the sand with rocks, we click at our captives with our tongues, like real wranglers do.

We fill the still morning air with our shrill whinnying. Mom, hanging wet laundry on the line, can hear us in the distance. She knows where we are. She is amused by our horseplay, but she does not laugh at us then, as she does now, when, in middle age, we can still greet each other with a playful whinny or a throaty nicker.

And now I chuckle too, when I recall Patsy's first date, a young Marine who walked all the way from the Base to see her, unaware that inside this teenage girl lurked a wild filly, who could flare her nostrils with rage and blast the air with a voice of triumph as she cantered proudly and defiantly through the desert.

Looking up at the night sky, we sit on the patio and gaze into the immense blackness punctuated with the twinkling of a trillion stars. We can see them all in the dark desert sky. The constellations stand out clearly against deep space, no illumination from city lights dimming the heavens.

Cassiopeia, Andromeda, Orion's Belt, The Big Dipper, the sprawling Milky Way. The words themselves an ancient chant. They form on Uncle's lips like secret passwords. He tells stories from mythology. In my childish awe, I believe he has experienced these myths personally. He knows them all so well.

Dad, in his own childlike vision, convinces us we are watching the satellites, Sputnik and Telstar, crossing the skies above us.

"See how they blink and move across the sky in their orbit?"

Yes, we see them. We see Dad's satellites as clearly as we see Uncle's archer releasing his arrows across the heavens. We look up into the night sky, deep into the infinite universe, until our necks ache and our eyes blur from looking so long and hard.

Mom brings out dessert. Chocolate chip ice cream in clear glass bowls. I prop my knees up in my chair and cradle the dish in my lap, attentions diverted from the stars' perpetual journey above us.

We are earthbound once again.

A few cumulus clouds are forming towers out to the west and southwest. We are hopeful. We want to feel the big stinging raindrops on our bare arms, to hold our palms over our ears to deafen the loud thunder claps that always follow after the blinding lightning bolts that zigzag in golden metallic Reddi Kilowatts across the dark skies. We can already smell moisture in the air. The greasewood is the first to issue the scent that promises rainfall.

We dash excitedly into the house and strip in a frenzy, pulling on our bathing suits in anticipation of the downpour.

Outside, around the tetherball pole with the round cement base scratched with all our names, we begin our rain dance. Our bare toes scuff up the dust. Skinny legs hopping in a dance that is a unique cross between an Indian beat and an Irish jig, arms swaying, voices shrill. Whooping and ay-yi-ing.

The rain clouds gather to the west, to the south, to the north, encircling us. But still the hot sun beats down on our circling rain dance. More often than not, the clouds skirt around us, tracking along the mountains, leaving us hot, sweaty and disappointed.

Now a sudden cool wind whips out of the violent skies, raising the hairs on our arms, shrinking the skin tight against our bones. The skies darken to a battleship grey and huge raindrops pelt down, popping the white dust in pellets about our legs. The winds gust angrily as we dance wildly with the thunderstorm. Eyes closed, tongues flat against our lower lips, mouths stretched wide open, we tilt our chins skyward to receive...

A cloudburst followed by flash flooding is a call to the washes that spill onto and across Pinion Drive, the waters carving out an age-old pathway, coursing downhill, curving and rushing. The violence of weather beyond control excites me, makes me humbly grateful for the sheer power of it.

"When Indian Cove gets a cloudburst, even if we don't get a drop of rain right here, we'll have a flash flood," Dad always said.

And so, at the first sign of thunderheads out to the west, we get ready to play in the nearby washes. Without any flood control to direct and divert the waters into manmade unnatural culverts, the sand rolls in powerful taupe-colored waves, a yellow creamy froth icing the muddy waters with a bubbly foam that cakes on our bare legs like melted frosting.

Standing on a sandbar, I watch the cream-and-coffee colored waters gushing past. Suddenly the sand base I stand on is ripped out from under me and I am thigh deep in the current. It is frightening and exhilarating. We all are shrieking in high voices, our emotions running as high and rampant as the wild waters we play in. Brush dances by, uprooted and bobbing along in the uncontrolled choreography of the floodwaters. At the time, we never give a thought to the unearthed snakes that are probably whipping along in the waters too, for we never see them, and so, do not fear them, as we romp and splash in the swirling froth.

When the currents subside, stranded cars are often discovered at road crossings, the waters having engulfed them, the drivers abandoning them in haste.

The floods unearth another play zone for us in the newly carved out banks of the washes. From the limestone clay, green and cool, we mold Indian pots and beads, etching designs in the damp clay with sharp sticks. We set our artwork in the hot sun to bake and harden before carrying them home to display gallery-style on the patio block wall, a child's tribute to that wondrous event called "flash flood."

Often the force of an electrical storm knocks out a transformer and leaves us without power. In the darkness we dig excitedly in the recesses of the kitchen drawers for candles, which we light and carry ceremoniously from room to room.

The candlelight casts a mysterious glow to our faces and throws bouncing monster shadows against the coarse plaster walls of the living room where we all huddle together. As the winds outside howl their rage, in the amber lit dimness stories are generated…

"I was only six years old when we left Germany," Mom narrates. "We came on a big ocean liner, your Aunt Lina, Oma and I. Papa had found work doing decorative work in a church in Vermont through a cousin who lived there. He had sent for us earlier, but Lina was engaged and refused to leave Bonbaden. But then she and Karl had a fight and broke up, so she wrote to Papa and asked him to send the tickets after all."

And so it was. The break up of a romance brought us to America. Not war, not a potato famine, not a Holocaust or political injustices, but a broken heart. Two broken hearts, for it was the early death in 1921 of my grandmother Lisette, from what was called "brain fever" during a flu epidemic, that caused the mourning Karl Bender to leave his well-respected photography and interior decorating studio, and the house on Jagerstrasse in Bonbaden, where my mother and her sister Lina were born.

Karl Bender settled in Niagara Falls and married a German immigrant, Augusta, who bore him another daughter, my mother's half-sister, Evelyn. But the impacts of trench warfare during WWI and the lingering grief over the death of Lisette, left Margotchen an orphan at age ten. In 1930 Karl Bender died at the early age of 42.

"It was the Depression," Mom continues in the hush of the candlelight. "My step-mother worked at the Shredded Wheat factory, so every night that is what I ate for dinner. I slept in a bed downstairs in the cellar, lying at my grandmother's side, crying myself to sleep with Oma's words soothing my dreams. "Not to worry, Margotchen. God takes special care of orphans."

The Immigrant

Margot looks at herself in the mirror.
A new haircut.
More severe than her usual softly curled, lightly teased short hairdo,
with feathered bangs framing her pale blue eyes.
Peachy silver grey coloring.

Skin Nivea-creme smooth,
with pleasant laugh lines at the corners of her eyes.
Intelligent. Alert. Sociable and friendly.
Eyes rich with memories.

She blinks and takes a long look at her new haircut.
Too short.
Cut close over her ears,
giving her a raised eyebrow intensity.
Too severe, she frowns.

Tears suddenly blur her blue eyes.
In the mirror she sees eight year-old Margotchen,
with soft brown hair, newly cropped short.
Like a boy's.

She sidles self-consciously into her school desk,
avoiding the harsh glares of the other students.
A German girl growing up in the La Salle district.
Niagara Falls, New York. 1928.
Trying to assimilate.
Losing her accent and walking tall.
A small child wanting to be accepted and admired.

And now? Her stepmother has chopped off her long, soft brown hair
into a conspicuous boyish bob.
"Immigrant," scold the eyes of her fellow classmates.
"My father killed Germans in the War,"
a group of boys harasses,
as she stoops to pick wildflowers on her walk home from school.

The woman blinks back her tears and hides her shorn hair
under her wrinkled hands.
Suddenly feeling old.
Her life's achievements clouded momentarily
by a glance in the mirror.

An immigrant, with a new haircut.

Entranced by our mother's impromptu tales, and with the electrical power not yet restored, we snuggle in for more...

"In the winter your dad's father would freeze over his back yard to create a pond and the whole 79th Street gang of neighborhood children gathered at the Spangenberg house for ice skating. I had no skates of my own, so I would beg your dad, "Joey, can I borrow your skates?" One December he got a new pair of skates for his birthday, so he gave me his old pair, those black hockey skates I still wear when we go skating up in Big Bear."

As the storm winds continue to buffet the windows, Mom continues her story.

"Tante Rosa, my step-mother's sister, had been transported Down Under in the early 1900s, where she served as governess to the Durechts, a wealthy Australian family. When the lady of the household died, Rosa married Mr. Durecht, and later resettled back in Niagara Falls. My father and Augusta bought their home on 79th Street from Tante Rosa, who was now herself a wealthy widow woman. She lived in a home with beautiful stained glass windows and a huge wood stove. Tante Rosa was always kind to me. She taught me how to embroider and she was a very good cook.

"When the word came from the hospital that my father had died, I was the one who answered the telephone. It was a chilly October day and I can still remember the thin dress I was wearing as I ran the three blocks to Tante Rosa's with the awful news."

The web of connection gathering us to our future desert home is entwined in Tante Rosa's friendship with the McFarland family, who owned the hardware store in the La Salle district of Niagara Falls. In the later '30s Tante Rosa made a trip out to California to visit Ernie McFarland who had moved to Manhattan Beach. Our mother was now living in Wilmington with her older sister Lina and her husband Pat, who had been transferred by the Customs Service from Detroit to the Los Angeles Harbor.

"Lina and Pat became great friends with Ernie. We had great times with them and their friends, who worked for the movie studios and lived in Burbank. We often joined them for weekend picnics and boating on a lake."

And, as the web continues its weaving in perpetual circles of connection, Ernie McFarland was married to Evelyn King's sister. And who was this Evelyn King? Evelyn and Burt King were part of the link to our family's eventual pilgrimage to Twentynine Palms.

In 1954, when Dad joined Mom, Patsy and me at the duplex, he found work delivering propane for Burt King, who owned the local Petrolane business. And so the desert connection became the Spangenberg story.

As well as story hours, the crack of lightning and deafening thunder that knocks the power out also creates the need for impromptu supper parties. With cooking pots and grocery sacks in hand, our neighbors, the Pavelkas, arrive at the door to borrow our stove, because they have electric and we have propane. Jean cooks up her unusual specialty, VandeCamp beans and bacon sandwiches and unending pitchers of multi-colored Kool-Aid.

When a tornado-like funnel cloud ripped through the desert, the Pavelkas' dog Tippy went wild and bounded through our kitchen door for safe haven as well. Part St. Bernard and Llewellyn Setter, big gentle Tippy gifted me with a lifelong love of the companionship of dogs and introduced me to life's cycles of birthing and dying...

In the cool of morning Raggedy Ann gives birth to her first litter of puppies fathered by big ole Tippy. In the planter box, sweetened by the scent of mint leaves mashed beneath her brown scraggly curls, I watch Raggedy Ann tug at several wet, dark bags that pulse out of her body.

Puppies emerge. Beautiful little puppies with blinded eyes, damp white fur and pink lips. Licking, so much licking— Raggedy Ann knows right away how to take care of her new babies. Patsy picks one out to keep. Isabel, named after a character in a novel my mother is reading at the time.

Who could shoot a dog? A big, gentle lovable dog like Tippy? Why?

There is no answer. But Elwin Pavelka finds his children's lost dog in a wash with a bullet hole in his big loving heart.

It is the first time I see a grown man cry. We watch our friends' father dig a hole for the family dog and lay him tenderly in his grave, while we hum and sob and pet Tippy one last time before covering him up with the cool earth.

Some time later we watch Elwin's coffin being carried out of Blessed Sacrament Church to a 21-gun salute. He has fallen asleep at the wheel on his long drive home through the dark desert from the Supply Depot in Barstow. Gentle and friendly, just like Tippy, Elwin's death is the end of the Pavelka era, for shortly afterward Jean, Patsy, Michael and Tommy move away to Florida.

Letter to the Editor of "The Desert Trail"
January 24, 1991

Dear Editor,

    I am very saddened to learn of the City Council's recent approval of a commercial project right across from the Oasis of Mara.

    I grew up in Twentynine Palms and consider it my home. My self-identity is derived from my childhood connection to that expanse of desert near my parents' homestead. I've spent many hours there, playing games, running free like wild horses, making "Indian" pottery from the clay soil in the washes, pondering decisions big and small, walking off a rage, listening to the wind, observing wildlife, or sitting alone in the solitude just to think.

    Just recently each of us five siblings fled into this familiar sanctuary to privately grieve the loss of our dad, who brought us to our desert home some 38 years ago. Our personal connectedness with this land continues, even though adult endeavors have taken us away from Twentynine Palms.

    I fear for the loss of the migrating buzzards, whose awesome arrival in the skies above the oasis signals the beginning of fall; the jackrabbits and cottontails whose whimsical criss-crossing of the desert amused us as kids; those beautiful white lizards who so enjoyed munching on my dad's precious garden seedlings; those skinny, blue-bellied lizards; the unexpected splash of brilliant yellow when a wild canary lights in the grey-tan brush, and the coo-coo-coo of a quail family.

    It's a shame this new developer couldn't put his creative ideas to work within the existing commercial district. Why set a precedent for commercial development in this unique oasis landscape?

    If there is even a glimmer of possibility to renege on the approval of this project, I hope there is a local group of citizens who can organize to overturn the Council's short-sighted decision.

    There are already plenty of Californians who have no idea what the native vegetation in their neighborhoods should look like. I hope in the future the Council will be more in tune with the unique and fragile beauty of the high desert and vote to preserve it.

Chris Spangenberg Carson
Los Olivos, CA

Not long after moving into our home on Cottonwood Drive, I had my first encounter with the disrupting force of "progress."

Patsy and I considered the empty fields across the street to be ours. After all, they were criss-crossed with our imaginary horse trails and our neatly piled rocks that marked the entries to our pastures and our corrals. No one else wandered there. The land was ours. The bushes were there for us to leap over. The gentle white lizards lounged in the sun for us to admire, or they darted hastily from our path when we decided to become lizard hunters.

The land stood undisturbed where it had always been. Beneath the blaze of desert sunshine, the land baked silently. Beneath the whistling winds that ripped the dusty top layer through the skies, the land lay still. Beneath a delicate dappling of snow, the land rested. The land. As it always was.

One day a skip loader shook the land from its constancy. Scraping. Tearing roots. Leaving the unresisting land bald and bare and perfectly flat. A house was being built.

Mom and Dad knew Jim Worth, the builder. They could be our advocates and ask him not to disrupt our playing fields, couldn't they? Jim was a nice man. He gave me my parakeet, Hey-You, and he always chats so friendly at the kitchen door during his break time, with his wide smile and kind brown eyes behind brown-rimmed glasses. He'd understand our wanting to keep our playing fields as they were. He'd want to save the field for us.

Not so, of course. The house went up. The stone piles lining our trails were strewn aside. The empty desert was being filled up. Another house went up soon after the first one. A neighborhood was slowly forming. It was irreversible. We learned that quickly. And, being adaptable as kids can learn to be, we turned our focus to the west, where acres of open desert lay untouched and timeless, stretching out as far as the Diagonal, the road that lead from town and fronted the Oasis, the boundary of the territory we were free to roam in.

This corridor of land, which was under consideration for commercial development by the City Council in 1991, as of this writing still stands vacant. An endangered landscape. Clump after clump, the grey-tan cattle spinach bush hunkers down in the harsh desert climate as it has for centuries, hosting the seen and unseen critters and plant life that depend on its constancy for their survival.

This seemingly insignificant parcel of land remains. Quiet, undemanding. Self-renewing. Self-regenerating. Necessary. As it always was.....*Sicut erat in principio, et nunc, et semper: et in saecula saeculorum.* As it was in the Beginning, is now, and ever shall be, world without end.

The land, as it always was. Carved, sculpted and re-shaped by rainfall and wind. Its fertility regenerated by unharnessed floodwaters spewing rich silt onto the receptive bosom of the valleys. The land, sheltering and breeding diversity, bearing the weight of mankind's treading footsteps. The land, groaning and suffocating silently under a foreign concrete skin.

Trip Time

Cars go by, droning into the distance.
Breaking up the air space.
I'm nestled between the pots and pans,
rolled haphazardly in a blanket
in the back of the Rambler station wagon.

The creek drips and tinkles.
Bleepy. Blippy. Bleepy. Blippy.

An airplane pushes aside the jet stream.
Rippling vibrating airwaves into my eardrums.

Bleepy. Blippy. Tinkle. Dripple.
The creek gurgles,
like a cat murbling a throaty purr.
A truck rattles by.
Sleep doesn't come.
Shoulders crack loudly deep between my ribcage.

Trip time in the station wagon.
Headed for Niagara Falls.
Sleeping beside the road amidst the camping gear.
Pots. Portable stove.
Blankets. Pillows.
Crayons and tablets.
"Navigation" maps.

My backseat bed partner shifts.
Kids' voices from a distant farmhouse tease.
Dad stands outside, leaned against the car,
looking.

The pepper tree shimmers in the breeze.
More cars drone past.
Electricity whines in overhead wires.
Hazy mountains shift silently...
stone on stone deep beneath the crusty earth.
Waves lap and slash at rocks, far, far beyond the mountains.

Crickets titter, one long brrrring.
Frogs repeat, repeat, repeat, repeat.
High in my ears.
Tinkle, dripple, blipple goes the creek.

The moon pushes away the darkening skies into a fuller circle.
Hear the heavens step aside
for the widening yellow cream arc?
Stars will soon blink on.
My eyes shut out the day's colors.
Breathing rhythms of sleep follow...

Trip time! Remember those words? Just the sound of them makes me giddy.

"Trip time!" Mom in her cotton nightgown rouses us from our sleep. Dad, with eyebrows raised humorously, chuckles as he gathers up the lantern, clothing bags and cardboard boxes of cooking utensils. He stuffs a grocery sack into one last crevice in the back of the car and we're off to the White Mountains in Arizona, one of Dad's favorite destinations. We can make it there in one day if we "push on through."

This time we don't make it in one day. Mom in the front seat, with baby Guy in diapers on her lap, has been suffering silently through our raucous harmonizing of "Soldier Boy" and "Big Girls Don't Cry-yi-yi." But as we pull into the dusty town of Apache Junction at dusk, she admits reluctantly that she has a terrorizing migraine headache and can't go one more mile.

Does this mean we get to stay in a motel? A rarity. My best buddy Kathy Walker has come along on this trip. Crammed into a station wagon with five other kids, it has to be a really novel experience for an only child, who is used to having the whole backseat of a Jaguar sports car to herself and has never been camping like this before!

Patsy, Kathy and I get our own room adjacent to the folks and the three boys. Heaven. A motel and our own room too! Our suitcases are part of Dad's intricate packed-up jigsaw puzzle, not to be disturbed. We don't want to waste any time, so we dash to the swimming pool and splash around in our wet blouses and shorts, diving off the side and practicing our Esther Williams water ballet kicks well into the darkness of the hot summer night.

The White Mountains hug the border of Arizona and New Mexico, a recreation area of pine forests that lies in the heart of an Apache Indian Reservation. The towns have names that ring like magical chants: Show Low, Pine Top, McNary, Big Lake. Here we pitch our big new blue tent and set up camp. We kids sleep outside in our bedrolls, where raccoons play underneath our cots and blue jays scold us unmercifully for occupying their territory.

Mom is an incredible camper. We never had a clue of her disdain for this type of vacation! She admits she hates camping only after we reach adulthood, when we can understand that in this pre-RV, pre-Pampers, pre-portable generator era, camping out with an infant or two was less than luxurious!

In her navy blue muu muu with the bright red and gold trim, Mom dances around the fire pit as gleefully as if she were in the Catalina Island Casino! She can cook like a chuckwagon pro on the green two-burner Coleman stove or over a rock-lined fire pit. Spaghetti with meat sauce, stew and delectable concoctions of C-rations from a can. Pancakes and bacon with hot chocolate and coffee to lure you from your nest in the chill of early morning!

With Dad, who likes to do things, we go off horseback riding through the woods or fishing at the shore of the lake. Or we "cruise the Bumble Bee on foot," which meant, taking a hike to the little market down the road with its wooden plank floors and crowded shelves. In the dark coolness of the market we spin the magazine stile, thumbing through the pages of teen magazines and crossword puzzle books, buying handfuls of Double Bubble Gum, Butterfingers, Big Hunks and chewy white waxy tubes filled with colored sugar water.

On our very first excursion to the White Mountains, we discovered the lumber mill compound of McNary, a company town with one incredible general store staffed by "real" Indians. Everything was sold in this place, from denim jeans and flannel shirts, ground chuck and soda pop, to shovels, wrenches and rubber-soled work boots.

At the shore of Big Lake we set up camp. Patsy and I in our sleeping bags under a pine tree where Dad had rigged up hammocks for us, so we could be up off the ground. Mom and Dad and the little boys slept in the car.

After our first night in this idyllic forest site, thunderclouds rolled in, followed immediately by an incessant downpour.

"It's just an afternoon mountain shower. It'll pass," Dad reckoned optimistically.

The cloudburst became a hailstorm. And when the hail turned to frosty snowflakes, we hastened to dismantle our camp at top speed and headed out of the White Mountains for drier territory. By late afternoon we had reached the Grand Canyon, which Dad had never seen before.

"Let's stop at this lookout, Dad!" we begged at each turnout.

"No, we'll have all day tomorrow to look at it. Let's find a campsite first."

"Please, here's another viewpoint!"

But, no, Dad was intent on setting up camp, getting the tent up before dark. While he played with the Erector Set of poles and riggings for the tent, Mom proceeded to make supper. No sooner had the corn been poured into the pan, when a boom of thunder greeted us, followed by giant pounding raindrops that quickly filled the cooking pots, drenching the camp cook.

As quickly as the tent was going up, the tent was coming down. Dad had had it. We were heading home. Grand Canyon or no Grand Canyon, we were on our way home!

Dad didn't see the Grand Canyon until some thirty years later, when our cousin Claudia from Germany came for a visit. Then, the vivid memories of corn kernels floating in a pan of rainwater made for a humorous and exaggerated storytelling epic, as trip-time memories always do.

Trip time! The memories roll behind my eyelids like the pavement beneath us as we pass through friendly little towns on two-lane roads...

Lunches made in the car. Fresh rolls spread with butter and topped with slices of ham, cheese, and tomato. Hand-picked peaches from roadside stands in St. George, Utah. Avocado and lemon juice on saltine crackers. A scroungy stray puppy dog that begs to come home with me in Wickenburg, Arizona.

Herbal scented green dinosaur soap from the gas station.

These cross-country trips take us past "the faces" in the Black Hills of South Dakota, with stop-overs at Wall Drug Store, through spooky mist-shrouded woods in Missouri, to a lakeshore in Rheinlander, Wisconsin, where yellow jackets attack little Mark, swelling his eyes shut into mere slits, and to "Gramma" Handschild's big farmhouse in the wide expanse of the Iowa corn belt.

As we drive along, Patsy and I count cars, keeping track of the numbers and types of automobiles we pass on slips of scratch paper with our elaborate cataloguing system: four straight lines and a slash, four straight lines and a slash. Ford, Buick, Plymouth, Chevrolet, Dodge, Nash, Desoto, International, Volkswagen, Studebaker. Each of us trying to be first to identify an oncoming car in our improvised trip game that occupies the hours on the road.

"You be the navigator, I'll be the pilot!" Dad would say in his Navy lingo. How I learned to love reading the maps, tracing our travels on lines of blue, summing up the miles between red dots, as we ventured eastward from brown, to green, to white, to blue spaces on my navigation charts!

"He needs rings!" Dad diagnoses whenever we pass a car spewing white smoke. "Uh-oh! They've got vapor lock," Dad observes when he spots a stalled car on a steep grade. "Don't let the scissor bird cut off your fingers!" he warns when we stick our hands out the windows to let them flop freely in the air. "This is the last trip we're taking!" he threatens, once again, when backseat bickering sets in.

Bright orange signs signal delays for the endless road construction of the late '50s and early '60s. We take detours on dusty by-ways, while giant earthmovers crash through the landscape to create the Interstates, highways that soon bypass the uniqueness of Small Town, USA, and all the colorful characters who live there. We could not foresee that fresh homemade pies and fried chicken would soon be traded for cardboard burgers at an ubiquitous fast-food joint and the duplicated strip malls and minimarts that would spring up to create the faceless towns of Cloneville, USA.

Three times as kids we traverse the broad landscapes of America, travelling clear across country on a shoestring budget, to return to Dad's birthplace, Niagara Falls, New York.

In contrast to our own wide-open patio surrounded by shadowy, story-sparking nightscapes and capped by an eternity of deep-space starlit skies, folks in Niagara Falls spend their evenings screened into porches encapsulated by low ceilings. Rather than gazing up into the vast night sky, here we look out horizontally at passers-by on the street.

We sit at wicker tables and learn to play Chess. Rather, I am allowed to watch, picking up the moves and memorizing them as the older kids manipulate pawns, queen, king and rooks on the checkered playing board.

Here, not far from the roar of the Falls, Mom and Dad first met as children. It was a neighborhood of German immigrants and "the Italians," who, to my Grandmother's obvious disdain, hung their laundry outside on balconies and flung their drapes wide open. I never understood why it annoyed her so, when we'd pull back her curtains like we did at home. I couldn't make the connection why she disliked these Wops, as she called them, who were simply letting the light shine in!

Although I only met my grandmother a few times and have no first-hand relationship to go by, her name was always spoken with such a harshness to the voice, that I think of her unfairly as spoiled, stern, intent on having her own way, irritable and feisty. Whenever one of us burped or sneezed too loudly, my mother would say, "Helen!" So what was I to gather, except that Gramma Helen was somewhat coarse, and not especially fond of my mother. I sense that she was envious, thinking of her daughter-in-law as sophisticated and snobbish, because she was better educated and had become a Californian.

"Who the hell is that?" Helen asked Dad, when I got out of the front seat of the car in her driveway. At age 16, after three days on a very long road-trip just to see her, when I could be home with my new boyfriend, this was some greeting! Now it seems quite humorous, because, for all I know, she might have been thinking I was Dad's girlfriend, and where was Margot?

With Uncle Hank, Dad's older brother, we take an outing on the Maid of the Mist, donning heavy yellow raincoats and slipping frighteningly close to the bottom of the roaring falls, the mist sprinkling us with a taste of the water's power, the noise deafening. At the top of the falls, only slim railings and blacktop paths separate us from the alluring waters.

Magnetizing, the power of the water pulls me to it. "Over the falls in a barrel?" Who are those reckless souls who have dared such an adventure? "I used to swim in this river," Dad said. Hard to believe. The force of the current is greater than I'd ever experienced or imagined.

We tour Great Aunt Rose's speak-easy on the Niagara River, hiding in the three-foot thick walls, and visit Great Aunt Mary, ill with diabetes, who remains in my memory as a frail, thin stick figure in pale blue clothing, while Great Aunt Tillie stands straight and strong at 6-feet tall.

In a cubbyhole under the eaves, we sleep in Dad's old room in the attic, a dusty, musty, cramped and secretive spot, while downstairs, Grampa hunches in front of the television set. My last memories of him are black and white images of his thin, bony torso stooped, from years of contorted postures as a plumber, I supposed, as he watches the Presidential convention on a dim TV screen, waving his fist and spouting a running commentary on this so-and-so and that. And Grampa's hand in mine as we walk on a grassy knoll in North Tonawanda to watch the fireworks.

Sisters of Mercy

All the sisters of mercy, they are not departed or gone.
They were waiting for me when I thought that I just can't go on.
And they brought me their comfort and later they bought me this song.
Leonard Cohen, 1967

From Sligo they came, out of the emerald green hills of the misty, moisty planet of Ireland. The five women stepped firmly onto the sun-bleached terrain of the Mojave Desert, their fair eyes squinting in the morning sunshine that splashed upon them. Dancing rays of light reflected and refracted from the grainy surface of the white-on-white sandscape, absorbing into the heavy black layers of cloth that wrapped their slender porcelain-white bodies, penetrating their damp pores and branding them as desert dwellers.

From the convent chapel their high sweet voices floated rhythmic Latin chants into the stillness, filling the desert air with new birdsong.

Magnificat! Anima mea Dominum. Et exultavit spiritus meus. "My soul doth magnify the Lord and my spirit doth rejoice in God my Savior."

The soft lilting voices of the Sisters of Mercy filled the air currents with morning prayer and late afternoon vespers, and filled our beings with a grand new Light.

Introibo ad altare Dei. Ad Deum qui laetificat juventutem meam. "I will go into the altar of God. The God of my gladness and joy."

In 1956 Blessed Sacrament School opened and, at the magical age of reason, I was formally introduced to the altar of God. Located just a block up the street from our home, the Church and School were to become an integral part of my young life. At Blessed Sacrament my social, spiritual and intellectual development sprang, evolved, festered, bloomed, rebelled; has been revoked and restored, has circled back and out from that source.

Blessed Sacrament.

O Lord I am not worthy, that Thou shouldst enter under my roof. Age-old prayers ascend into the holy water dampened air, recited in a Zen-like trance from the rote memory of childhood. Beams of sunlight stream through stained glass portraits of the saints, diffusing into a wash of aqua, pink and violet. Hands folded, face serious, angelic and pious, I count the massive beams in the church ceiling until they fade into a blurred canvas of grey-tan imagery...

Up at the pulpit Patrick J. O'Dowd, the agent of God the Father, rocks back and forth on his heels; his right-hand woman, Mother Cyril and her Irish troupe of nuns—Sisters Mary Margaret, Mary Josephine, Teresa—figures, soft and stern, are imprinted in my memories with an indelible ink of ritual, discipline, honor, respect and tradition.

At Blessed Sacrament School no electronic buzzer goes off impersonally at a pre-programmed moment to summon us to the blacktop for the daily morning recitation of the Pledge of Allegiance, but a large brass bell held firmly in the grasp of Mother Cyril's thin white fingers. She seems to need the strength of her entire shoulder and neck to ring the bell with such loud, unquestionable authority.

No matter how intense the moment of a softball game's run around the bases; nor if you are just so very close to beating Ralph Theis for the first time ever in a foot race; no matter if your swing is about to beat all records for the highest, farthest bail-out of all attempts thus far, when that bell rings, all activity ceases and the march back to the classroom takes precedent. Girls in faded blue jumpers and pixie caps with gold rings to hold the hat into a tail, and boys in white shirts that refuse to stay tucked into grey cotton pants, stand, sit or kneel with a stillness foreign to today's youth. Quietly we sit at our desks, "on our honor," when Sister leaves the room, our guilty faces cast downward as she suddenly reappears at the door.

Sister Mary Josephine strides down the rows of desks, her wooden pointer tapping out the rhythm of multiplication tables, imbedding them permanently into our memory. And for choral recitation she arranges us in a group at the front of the room. Holding our chins high and proud, just as she holds her own pointed features, we stand tall and straight, eNUNciating each line with exaggerated protrusion of our lips for the vowels, t's and p's sharply and distinctly spit out, as we recite, "The owl and the PUSSYcat when to SEA, in a BEAUTiful pea green BOAT..."

All during second, third and fourth grade, I sit at my desk, longing to become an altar boy, as Sister Mary Josephine puts the squirming young lads through their training. *Ad Deum qui laetivicat juventutem meam...* Why can't those boys remember anything? I know all the words and all the moves! How and when to carry the cruets for the priest to wash his hands of all his iniquities, when to ring those magnificent golden bells at the Consecration, when to bow, when to sit, when to stand. Let me be an altar boy!

Every moment of Catholic school is infinitely thought provoking! The Angel of the Lord declared onto Mary. And she conceived by the Holy Ghost. The words of the Angelus precede our lunch hour, so, with much food for thought, I walk home at noon to enjoy Mom's left-over pot roast or cottage cheese and jam sandwiches and to share with her my tirade of all the injustices I've been handed out that morning: how Kathy finked on me for not wearing socks, the infamous note I got caught passing to Philomena accusing Mother Cyril of reading to us like we were babies, how Leonard called me names I didn't know the meaning of for not reading his Valentine right away, or how Laura was chosen for the part of Mother Mary for the May procession and why not me?

Choir practice is a large part of the school day. Sister Mary Margaret, the sweet nun, with her kind face and quiet way, leads us in song with her beautiful voice. Lenten hymns, solemn and soul-searching. *Pange lingua gloriosi, corporus mysterium....* Gregorian chants of the Kyrie and the joy of the Gloria.

We clomp up the stairs to the choir loft and peer down at the pews below, imagining the terror of falling over the railing onto the unsuspecting congregation below. The one-time honor of being selected to direct the choir feeds a fantasy career of conducting an orchestra even though I play no instrument!

Bless this house, O Lord we pray...that one day we may dwell, O Lord, with Thee. How could a solitary desert child even conceive of thriving in a heaven filled with throngs of human spirits? "But, are there horses in heaven?" Patsy wants to know!

There's a crimson banner flying.
There's a crimson flag unfurled.
For the knights of Christ are marching
To the conquest of the world.

— "Holy Childhood" anthem

In her long flowing blue parachute Patsy stands at the dresser in our shared bedroom, her back to me as she raises her cupped hands to the ceiling, playing "priest." Flattening a piece of soft white bread into a round mashed circle, her silken cassock rustles as she pronounces, "This is my Body," and genuflects, hands resting on the dresser as she bows humbly yet ceremoniously.

Standing up again she grasps Mom's royal blue bottle of Nivea hand lotion and lifts it above her head, elbows locked. "This is the Chalice of my Blood," she says, stifling a laugh, as she spots her pious freckled face in the mirror. Gaining her composure she turns to face her congregation, me, posture straight and face angelic, a rolled-up towel serving as a kneeler, with a backdrop of metal bunk beds rising up behind me like a celestial choir loft.

Spreading her folded hands apart, Patsy gestures wide. "*Dominus vobiscum.*"

Next I stand with eyes downcast and hands folded at the closed closet door, examining my conscience for the many sins I have committed during the past week. Penitent I kneel, mining my memory for moments of misdemeanor. Inside the closet Patsy fusses with the bulk of her vestments, pulling the swishy parachute fabric with its mass of cords from under her knees. She yanks open the sliding metal door, her face hidden behind a hanging pair of trousers.

"Bless me, Father, for I have sinned," I stammer weakly. Long silence.

"Ahem," the priest clears her throat. "Yes?"

"I missed my morning prayers twice. I, uh, ate this extra delicious hot dog at Friday's football game, with Dad. I think I thought an impure thought..."

"Impure thoughts. Hmmmm," the priest titters, jostling more hanging clothes around her. "Can you describe these thoughts you've been entertaining?"

"No, I don't think so."

"You've been looking at that photo, I bet," the priest says slyly. "You know, that black and white one you got at the drive-in, the one with Elvis on the sofa with that beautiful dark-haired girl with long eyelashes, and she's leaning way back in her tight, short dress, and she has this look in her eye and her teeth are even chattering, and he's got his hand on her waist, and she's looking at his mouth, and, gads, he's gonna kiss her, and I get all jiggly inside..."

"Three Hail Mary's, three Our Father's, and three Glory Be's," the priest says grimly through locked teeth, suddenly realizing she, the priest, has just exposed her own "impure thoughts."

Patsy slams the closet door shut with finality, chuckling to herself in the darkness of the closet, as I suddenly burst out of the room, rap desperately at the closed door of our only bathroom, and wet my pants in hysterical laughter as a fatherly voice says, "I'm in here."

Somberly, I return to the chapel and flop down flat on the bedroom floor. I close my eyes and lie there still as a corpse. Opening a jar of Vick's "giggle rub," Patsy anoints my chest and forehead with the oils of Extreme Unction. "Rest in peace," she says solemnly, making the Sign of the Cross in the air above my face.

Together we stand at the mirror. "Holy Go-odd, we prai-ase Thy name," we sing as high and schrieky as we can, mimicking Lucille Baskerville's soprano choir voice, closing our religious ritual with a final hymn of Benediction.

The voices are always there. In the rhythm of the jump rope, tapping, tapping, tapping on asphalt. Keep the beat. 2 one's 2. Jump. Tap. 2 three's 6. Jump. Tap. 2 five's 10. Jump. Tap. Pride, covetousness, lust. Jump. Tap. Anger, gluttony, hatred, revenge. Jump. Tap. Drunkenness and bad example. Jump. Tap.

The hand turns the rope. Listen for the circular sound of the wrist twisting in the spiraled light waves, bouncing along the contours of the knuckles.

The swamp cooler hums. Its current bops against the rhythm of my heart's own electric muscle. Pushing me out of step, out of sync.

The voice informs me, "Confirmation is the sacrament through which the Holy Spirit..."

...through which I can receive the sound waves if I stand way out in the desert and just listen. For surely if I stand in the stillness and stretch out my arms like receptor bat wings, the throbbing vibrations of the swamp cooler pressing through the classroom window can penetrate way out there, if I just listen.

"Do you know the answer?" she asks.

"No, I don't."

"I bet if I asked you about something else you'd have the answer."

What did she mean? What answer? What something else?

Standing at attention at the back of the room, I lick my lips and stare at the condensation on the cooler pads, at the beads of sweat collecting on Mother Cyril's furrowed brow.

What does she mean, what something else?

How Arthur's muscled butt fills his grey cotton uniform slacks bobbing up and down in his tip-toe gait? How legs look better without socks to break up the smooth line where ankle and calf meet? How two bodies get so warm they could easily melt together when we have our contest to see who can dance the closest at Kathy's driveway party?

What? What answer is she referring to? What something else? What answer do I have that she wants to know?

Charity, joy, peace, patience. Jump. Tap. Benignity, goodness, longsuffering, mildness. Jump. Tap. Faith...

The voices are always there.

Et introibo ad altare Dei. I go into the altar of God, into the Oasis of Mara, where I come to perceive, wordlessly, the real presence of the Divine. In the Oasis, amidst the tall, sweet greenness of the grasses fed by hidden underground springs, beneath the lone charred "matchstick" palm tree, on hands and knees in the mesquite tunnels or astride the fallen "balance beam" palm tree, there, in the lushness of the Oasis, in the stillness of the desert air, I experience the soul-and-body pervasiveness of power and beauty, strength and serenity, and an unparalleled source of Goodness.

In the heat of summer the cool shadows of the giant cottonwood tree draw us to the western end of the Oasis. We scale the leaning trunk to hide in its dancing leafy canopy. Patsy's dog Lizzie climbs up the tree with us, gripping with her claws to perch like a tree monkey, nudging in close to keep us safe.

We hunker down low in the grasses or flatten our bodies to the shaded, leaf-littered earth, breathing in the rich dampness of the soil. Streaking our foreheads, cheeks and chins with mud, we crouch in the thorny mesquite caves. Warriors, listening to the quiet, looking out into the distant desert. Tense, ears alert. Noiselessly we pad barefoot in the brittle leaves Indian-style, the scent of blooming arrow weed filling our noses.

September finds us scanning the skies for the return of the buzzard migration. The giant birds soar on the high currents, a cloud of black wings, making a loose haphazard formation, then circling and circling, swooping downward to invade our Oasis playground, taking it over, dotting the palm trees with hundreds of black silhouettes. The Oasis then becomes the buzzards' occupied territory, for during their sojourn the air is permeated with the nose-wrinkling stench of carrion.

As we creep along the trails, the huge birds sit hunch-backed looking down at us, with their ugly bare neck skin and sharp claws, suddenly flapping their extended wings, startling us with an air-beating clamor. Black and ominous, the buzzards are the symbol of fall. As suddenly as their vast numbers fill the skies, we wake one morning and they are gone, and we will miss them until their return, for they always return, driven by the circular cycle of the seasons. Buzzards' breath, death. Buzzards' wings, life.

Fall brings a feeling of fatigue to the limbs, a weakness, as if the months of hot, hot days have sucked out my core of energy, leaving me inert and quiet, melancholy, looking inward. Sounds drone long and slow, shadows lengthen, and the creases in the mountains become sharply outlined, glowing pink and purple at sunset, the white sands in the basins of the black Bullion Mountains to the north reflecting peach and lavender. Waking on a winter morning, I sense a quiet, soft and pervasive. The living room is lit with a reflected glow of whiteness. Snow! Time to put on layers of clothes, three pairs of socks, a wild rummaging through drawers for mittens and Dad's woolen Navy sweater, not a minute to lose! No school today! It's snowing!

We work our way up to the Oasis, snowballs blasting, fingers reddened and frozen. Aching with the cold, we roll down the small mounded hills. The dust of snowy powder makes the thorny bushes and cactus unrecognizable until we tumble into them on our imaginary sleds. We roll as much snow as we can into icy mounds, poking broken sticks and the hollow tubes of hole-pocked cholla branches into the snowmen for eyes and noses. By mid-afternoon, our slender snow people have melted, rinsing away the protective coating from the millions of invisible flower seeds hidden in the wet grains of sand. Springtime will emerge, once again, painting the altar of God with a blush of colors.

Light and Shadow

"This is Margot Spangenberg from the Desert Trail." My mother is on the phone, interviewing people for the weekly column she writes for the local newspaper. 29 Palms Gazing. She does not know that I am listening and I am not aware that I am recording it all. Unconsciously memorizing the script, filing away the imagery, her style and grace.

She is a skilled writer and a cordial conversationalist, gathering the material for her articles, filling her green-paged steno pads with the secret language of her flowing, confident Shorthand notes. Pecking rhythmically and surely on the black and silver round flat keys of the old Underwood typewriter at the grey metal hulk of her bedroom desk. A tap dance of stories—Mr. Hayes' English rose garden, the blooming Century plant, social gatherings, births, travels and achievements of the locals.

For years I listen in the background to her phone interviews, watch her type her stories in time for deadline, measuring the column inches by which she is paid. I have absorbed it all.

And so I write too. News releases, community arts events, promotions and publicity, documentation of in-school arts workshops, profiles of local business people. Environmental newsletters. Trip adventures. And letters, lengthy and detailed, filled with everyday chatter. Poems. And diaries. Volumes of daily drib-drab and wonderings filling the pages. Journals that sit in dusty boxes in the garage. Fond recollections that bring me to laughter and unexpected tears, and sometimes revelations, when I chance upon them during cleaning binges.

It is the small, seemingly insignificant happenings and sharings of the Alltag that form our lifetimes and make us the rich, unique individuals that we are. Nothing is overlooked in our mindfulness. We record the way the soft light comes through the kitchen window weaving through the new green leaves of the peach tree, the crepe paper indigo flowers of the smoke tree in bloom, the deep purple-pink of the shadows on the Sheeps Pass Mountains at sunset, the mournful ku-koo-ku of the dove's call.

Dad's shoulders bobbing up and down when he laughs quietly with his toothy grin and smiling crystal blue eyes. Aunt Lina's deep-voiced "Good evening," spoken with an accented long extended "eee" as she enters the front door. Mother Cyril's famous aphorism, "Laziness, did I ever offend thee?" still ringing in my ears like the clanging of the large brass school bell held in her delicate white hands, hailing us into the classroom.

Long striding footsteps on the cement walkway late at night, keys jingling on a Sam Brown belt, patrol shift over. My long-limbed daughter rehearsing her gymnastics floor routine in the kitchen, the square floor tiles defining her balance beam. The smell of race gas at the motocross starting line, engines revving, tailpipes smoking, starting gate slamming to the ground—Patrick gets the hole shot! The crash of glass bottles being poured into the recycling truck on Monday mornings. A close friend's dark brown eyes filling to overflowing with tears emanating from her depths.

Gestures, tones and voices. Light and shadow. Sounds.

Nothing really goes unnoticed. We observe and connect without consciously knowing, taking little pieces of it all over time, becoming our Selves.

The Walkers

Kathy emerged from the back room of Walkers Dress Shop, where, as an only child, she entertained herself while her mother tended to her customers.

"You and Christy are going to be in Kindergarten together!" my mother said enthusiastically as way of introduction.

Kathy, in her own unabashedly forthright way, said, "Yuck!"

And so we became fast friends.

With a keen sense of humor gleaned from solitary afternoons watching Soupy Sales or the antics of Jackie Gleason, "The Life of Riley" and "Father Knows Best" and, of course, having a witty mother with a chuckle I can still hear to this day, no one could elicit tears-spilling-down-your-cheek laughter like Kathy. Whether miming a person flossing his teeth in the manner of Red Skelton, or mimicking a TV commercial—"Mars, heavenly Mars, toasted almond bars," while she munched her candy, Kathy was funny and fun to be with.

While I, the studious one, memorized Longfellow's somber words: "Tell me not in mournful numbers, life is but an empty dream. For the soul is dead that slumbers and things are not what they seem," Kathy stood up at the front of the classroom and recited quite confidently, "I loathe, abhor, detest, despise, abominate dried apple pies. The farmer takes his gnarliest fruit. 'Tis wormy, bitter and hard to boot."

Kathy thought up all sorts of ways to "get my goat." Inviting me up to her house on Serrano Drive for the best sandwich ever, which I was gullible enough to believe until I bit into the oily, noxious oyster-onion sandwich she had prepared. Or hiding a treasure box full of See's candy from me, where months later she finally revealed the hiding place on top of the kitchen cabinets, where the chocolate now languished green and moldy, dusty and inedible, a wastefulness unthinkable to me, sure to doom one to months in Purgatory!

Kathy and I donned Gladys' golden harem pajamas and matching jewel-studded slippers, lounging like desert goddesses on the carport asphalt. We concocted magic potions from a mixture of creams, lotions, perfume and tonics for the skin from Gladys' well-stocked make-up cabinet. We went through a brief playing-with-dolls phase, pretending to be doctors, delivering babies through our belly buttons.

We dined in fashion on frozen TV dinners set up on trays in the den, something never done at our house. We always sat down together for a homemade family meal with lively conversation and discussion, with the television definitely OFF. Even the Walkers' dogs had attitude. Asta, Kathy's feisty short-haired terrier, named after Nora's dog on "The Thin Man." Herman, the Dachshund, who almost drowned on a boating trip. And Hiram, a tall, wiry Airedale with incredibly bad breath.

I came to know the Walkers from the intimate vantage point of a child, observing, accepting and assimilating their personal ways without judgment or the weight of pre-conceived notions. In my childhood assessment of the strata of society, everything about the Walkers was "first class." Not in the "snubbing you uppetyness" of the Marine Corps Officers' kids, who wouldn't include you in their game of Marco Polo at the Club pool (an assumed status built into a system they automatically belonged to), but an innate sense of style and gentility worn without haughtiness or to the exclusion of others.

Gladys was the Marlene Dietrich of downtown Twentynine Palms, her voice throaty, her light brown hair softly curled, her posture like that of models in fashion illustrations, hips slightly forward, cigarette in hand, neck arched back, amused and amusing. As a merchant in a small, remote desert community Gladys offered quality women's clothing in the current stylishness of the day.

My mother's recollections best describe Gladys' knack of tactful persuasion and salesmanship. "You would go to her dress shop thinking you wanted a blue outfit, but Gladys would look you over with an appraising eye, go to the rack and bring out something yellow. 'Try it on,' she'd command. And I did, of course. Wow, there was a new you! So afterward you enjoyed compliments you'd never have gotten otherwise."

Kathy and I went along with Gladys to "market," as she called her seasonal expeditions to the Los Angeles garment district to select new ladies' wear for the store. From the swank Biltmore Hotel where we stayed overnight, we strode briskly down big city boulevards, through tunnels of high rise buildings and past preaching derelicts in Pershing Square. We wandered through racks and racks of clothing at Miss Pat, White Stag and other wholesale dealers, while Gladys shrewdly dealt with vendors in the language of fashion, fabric, styles and pricing.

At holiday time Kathy and I "helped out" with the gift-wrapping. Kathy had long ago mastered Gladys' exacting technique of looping the satiny ribbon into thick spirals, cutting a wedge-shaped notch in the center of the loops and securing the bow onto the package, separating the loops just so. But my bows were always lop-sided, the notch cut too deeply or raggedy, the resultant bow refusing to stand up straight and securely.

For some time I tried to replicate that perfect bow whenever I wrapped a gift, but finally resorted to my own signature gift-wrapping style, opting to tie lavender or whatever's blooming in the yard at the moment, with a straightforward piece of raffia instead!

I got invited along on all sorts of outings. Auto racing at the new Riverside Raceway. Jeep trips with Earl's buddies, Joe Staley and Denny Sermersheim, Gladys insisting we wear "car coats," as it got quite chilly bouncing around in the open air over hill and dale in Jack Rabbit Pass. To the Dodger Stadium at Chavez Ravine for a baseball game featuring the Angels and the Orioles. Until this time I'd been able to conceal my extreme near-sightedness, but, on handing back the binoculars to Earl, he exclaimed, "Can you see out of these adjusted like this?" Glasses soon followed!

Kathy and I boarded a Bonanza Airlines prop-jet for my first flight in an airplane. We flew from Palm Springs to Blythe to visit Uncle Palmer and Aunt Evelyn. Uncle Palmer owned a men's clothing store in downtown Blythe. At their home was a patio room separate from the main house with a wine cellar. Bottles lay slanted in clay pipes built into the stucco wall to keep cool. In the long summer afternoon, Kathy and I lit bunches of Gladys' Salem cigarettes that were stashed in a bronzed donkey statue. The cigarettes were dispensed out the tail-end, which was far more entertaining than pretending to be suave and nonchalant as we puffed away in a cloud of smoke, that alerted Gladys to ask, "Have you been smoking?" as she entered the room. Of course we answered, "Of course not!" Us, smoking? Why would she think that?

"In Ashfork we were stranded. We knew it when we first landed..." Gladys pens onto a sheet of motel stationery. She is instructing us on the many ways to use the diaries she has bought Kathy and me while we wait out the delivery of a fuel pump for Earl's grey-blue Jaguar sports car that has chosen to break down on a remote stretch of Arizona highway.

I can still picture Gladys in her white silk slip, legs crossed, toenails and fingernails polished a bright glossy red. She sits on the foot of the bed, early morning light streaming through a motel window somewhere in New Mexico or the panhandle of Texas, a halo of smoky haze forming above her as she drags on her cigarette. She takes a long slurp of the morning coffee she has brewed in the room and clears her throat in her five-syllable distinctive growl, accenting the final "hhhem" at the back of her throat.

We are enroute to Oklahoma where Earl's father, Uncle Orben and Gladys' mother all live. At Uncle Orben's farm Kathy and I ride on wayward donkeys that are intent on knocking us off, heading straight for the peach orchard, scraping us against the branches where we're sure to get "chiggers," worrisome, invisible little insects that we later scan our bodies nervously for when we shower.

We sit around the dinner table, Uncle Orben's tall, bony greyhound Popcorn at his side, and they all laugh when I speak to them in their own Oklahoma drawl, completely unaware that I have been listening and absorbing their soft language like a new song.

The Hilton in Albuquerque is the first hotel I ever stayed in. Up and down the elevator Kathy and I ride, pretending we live in the hotel like the storybook character, Eloise, ordering elaborate make-believe room service meals, traipsing through the lobby like it is our ordinary, ho-hum, everyday lifestyle. Saying "Lobby, first floor, sixth floor, please," to the elevator attendant who plays along with our charade.

Because Kathy gets carsick, she misses a lot of the scenery we pass through while she lay down in the backseat. I, on the other hand, sit straight up, "like a passenger on a train," Earl says, smiling back at me through the rear-view mirror, as we tour the southwest—Mesa Verde, Carlsbad Caverns, the White Sands of New Mexico and over the hills to Alamagordo and Tucumcari.

Spotting a wide spot in the road, Gladys would suddenly announce, "Pull over!" Earl pretended to act quite displeased as she swung open the passenger door and squatted in the shelter of the passenger door to "hang a half-moon," (Earl's own words for her actions)! And, as we wind our way up and around the curves to Pike's Peak, Earl gets quite a kick out of the anxious "Nooooo!" that I blurt out in reply, when Gladys asked Earl if he'd like another beer!

At a restaurant called The Chisholm Trail, somewhere in Texas, I suppose, Gladys insists that I am not to order another plain, old hamburger, but a real T-bone steak! The Walkers introduced me to all types of exotic foods—frog legs, venison, dove and quail breasts. Years later Gladys saw to it that my husband and I would acquire Earl's favorite hunting gun from his collection, an Austrian Mannlicher rifle, a memento of the man who was, to me, a combination of Chief Geronimo and John Wayne—quiet, kind, accepting, and wise.

As much time as I spent with them, in my shyness, I could never bring myself to call either Gladys or Earl by their first name. It seemed too presumptuous, too intimate somehow. They were both fully aware of my awkwardness about this, often trying to trick me into having to ask them for something. They called me "Christabelle," a name endearingly reserved for me, plain old me, who truly lacked anything close to style!

It always intrigues me what different memories people carry from their perspective of the past. Patsy remembers Kathy "ironing the money" at her mother's dress shop. Mom tells of Kathy pouting because she had to go to school with Sisters for teachers. And Kathy recalls that my mother always ate cottage cheese when she was pregnant with Guy. None of which I recall at all! But as the projector flickers on the final frame, I see Kathy and me dosie-doe-ing arm in arm, our shadows frolicking on the firelit boulders at Belle Campground, our adolescent laughter ringing in the desert night air.

Local Color

"It's Joan!"

And through the front door she whooshed like an exotic, brilliantly feathered bird, filling our simply furnished living room with dramatic energy.

An actress from the early Hollywood days, Joan Valerie had come to the High Desert to start a community theater, and had encouraged my mother to develop into a stage actress, with her debut to be a minor role in the opening production of "Father of the Bride."

See, Mom's column for The Desert Trail introduced her to all the local color. But Joan, with that theatrical lilt in her voice, was the most brilliantly colorful of all characters.

Dressed in violet and mustard gold, her dangling earrings flashing, I observed Joan like an Audobon bird watcher marveling at the sighting of a rare species on New Year's Day. Her skin was a smooth, sculpted bronze, with the glossy sheen of herbal oils. Her eyelashes were thick with black mascara, her lids painted in smoky lavender, mossy green or cobalt blue. The scent of perfumed oils wafted through our house for days after her visits.

Her bleached blond hair was pulled tautly back, so that her facial features and expressions stood out more pronounced. Reading glasses hung from a woven cord around her neck. And when she said my mother's name, Margot, the quality of her speech transformed the name into the stature of a goddess.

Joan ventured often down to Mexico for "treatments," and all the colors of Latin America seemed to migrate north on her return. She owned an adobe home in the Plaza, near the Fosters Freeze, and entering it was indeed like going into a small, walled Mexican hacienda. Inside it smelled of new-to-me culinary aromas from Joan's Greek heritage—spinach pie dripping with fruity olive oil, eggplant, oregano and garlic.

Joan became part of our family, as incongruous as that seems. On one of our summer vacation trips, we even rendezvoused with her in Rhinelander, Wisconsin, to meet her brother who owned a Greek restaurant there. And she brought interesting visitors into our home as well. Like the distinguished actor Felix Locher, who had the role of Joseph of Arimathea in "The Greatest Story Ever Told," which was being filmed at that time.

One afternoon we met up with Joan at the Smoke Tree Ranch in Palm Springs where Hollywood actors routinely vacationed. There Joan introduced Patsy and me to a man riding a beautiful Quarter Horse.

"Nice to meet you, Mr. Grant," we said politely. And Patsy, who was about 15 at the time, began to chat with him with fervor about horses and Western saddles and riding.

"Would you like to go along with us on a trail ride?" Mr. Grant offered.

"Oh, nooo!" Patsy answered emphatically. "We're going for ice cream and my mother has groceries in the car!"

My sister, oblivious to his stardom, the horse being the celebrity that intrigued her, had just turned down "an affair to remember" with Cary Grant, courtesy of our wondrous friend, the one-and-only Joan Valerie!

Fond Recollections

Whenever Carol spoke of King City, her lips spoke the words that gave us, her co-workers, a glimmer of her growing-up years, a taste of her past history. But the gaze in her eyes, the unconscious upturn of her mouth and her hoarse chuckles suggested far more vivid mind pictures than her sentences could ever portray.

When she spoke the names of familiar places—Jolon Road, Camp Roberts, Hunter Liggitt—her round fair face with its scattering of pale freckles became childlike, and I knew that behind her eyes she was far away, back in a magical moment of her own, wending her way through her private memories of high school jalopies, driving fast on dark, twisty backroads, carefree reckless teenage laughter careening off the night-blackened mountain ridges.

Now, as I pass through King City, after a long stretch of monotonous driving in the surreal dawn hours, I see the freeway exit marked "Jolon Road," and I too catch the magic of that word.

Carol's shared stories allow me to see more than just a neon-lit highway truck stop café and a four-corners town stuck in the middle of a dreary piece of endless blacktop.

I see Carol. Her face transformed by fond recollections of growing-up times, her eyes glazed by the magic of the suggestive words—Jolon Road, Hunter-Liggitt, Camp Roberts.

At 40-something you suddenly see where you've come from, and you can almost see where you're going. The looking back is filled with nostalgia, the total story glossed over with sweet-scented memories. The "good old times" and "remember when's" are fondly remembered with mixed tears of treasured recollection as well as a sense of loss. A simplicity of delight. A longing to recapture the awesomeness of childhood exploration, to see things once again for the first time, with a purity of discovery...

A tiny pink baby bird with a misshapen, purplish belly and huge yellow blank eyes. Fallen from its nest, we rescue the creature and try to save its life. With unabashed hopefulness we feed the featherless birdling with an eyedropper. Drip, drip, drip into the wide-open beak.

When the weak little bird finally dies, we tenderly place it on a bed of cotton balls, encase it in a white gift box and walk in funereal procession to the Oasis, where we dig a hole in the tree-shaded grassy slope, entombing the cardboard coffin in the dark, damp earth.

"Dust thou art, to dust returneth," we murmur together in the stillness of the early morning.

And, in the blissful recollection of childhood adventures, a reality leaks in, uninvited. Dad always wanted to move.

"Let's leave this God-forsaken place, this Nowheresville."

Locked in a job, not necessarily of his own true choosing, Dad was restless. Surrounded by huge bulletin boards dotted with colored paper strips and thumb tacks denoting schedules of repairs, additions, demolition, construction and pothole patching, Dad was Master Scheduler for the Marine Corps Base. If it broke, he decided when to fix it, which workers to send, what pieces of heavy equipment, electrical wiring, pipes and faucets to set in motion for the job.

The Master Scheduler in the Maintenance Department, Dad was a dreamer frustrated by an inability to frame his own master schedule for change. Family commitment, the responsibility of providing for five children, caring for others always took priority for Dad over his own needs or desires. Self-indulgence was not in his vocabulary.

Weekend jaunts to the mall three hours away in West Covina, fishing trips to Big Bear Lake and White Water, treks to Fedco in San Bernardino—were these excursions Dad's response to a chronic urge to get the hell out of here? Some unresolved restlessness?

All the same, they are outings lovingly recalled. Because, in his desire to escape, we all experienced an irreplaceable sharing of family togetherness, laughter and adventure, and an unparalleled fulfillment that showed in Dad's eyes every time he looked at us, loving us always, and wanting us to be happy.

His longing to explore new territory gave us trips clear across country, picnics and horseback rides, ice skating and tobogganing, rock climbing and shopping excursions. His restlessness fed his own adventurousness and ours. His imagination nurtured an ability to create fun out of the mundane.

If there were snow flurries in the Monument, we bundled up in mittens, wool socks, stevedore caps and jackets, grabbed blankets to wrap up in, and crammed into the car to be the first ones to put our footprints in the snow banks. We pulled off the roadway in the dark and got stuck in a pile-up of deepening snow. After a litany of Hail Mary's, shivering anxiously with our noses pressed against the frosty car windows, Dad dug us out on his hands and knees in the freezing slush, and we pushed on up the winding roadway—to find better snow!

We were a spontaneous crew. One Friday evening we were nestled cozily in our car, our fists filled with hot popcorn brought from home in butter-stained grocery sacks, watching "The Pink Panther" at the Starlite Drive-in Theatre.

Suddenly huge flames caught our attention to the south in the direction of the Oasis. Abandoning Peter Sellers and his blundering antics, Dad stashed our speaker back in its cradle and skidded in haste out of the drive-in parking lot to witness the live action in our own neighborhood.

The 29 Palms Inn was on fire!!

Mom had a press pass, so we were able to drive right up to the scene of the fire just as a support team of Marine Corps fire trucks arrived from the Base. With a whooping war cry, the men dragged their hoses to the flaming palm trees, as, wide-eyed with excitement, we watched the landmark inn scorch and burn in the night sky.

Mom had a "press pass." The law might call it "rubber necking," but we don't see it that way. Mom didn't have a real pass nor did she need one. Everyone knew Margot Spangenberg from The Desert Trail. She had stories to write. And whenever we could, we went with her to the scene of the action. To this day, whenever I hear a siren or see smoke, I still have the urge to grab my camera and be the first one on the scene, to witness first-hand what's happening, and to find my own words to document the momentous event.

The Shadow

I was Dad's tag-a-long, his quiet little shadow. I don't remember that we talked a lot as I accompanied him into town, down the sandy road to the Knights of Columbus Hall, or out to the Doblers' place to do refrigeration work on the milk delivery trucks. But he heard the unspoken child's request, "Can I be with you?" and so I went along with him, often. Just the two of us.

It's no wonder that I am perfectly at home in an auto repair shop, out in the garage with my son's motorcycle race gas permeating the air, puttering in the yard with rakes, wheelbarrows or shovels, or sorting through aisles of tools and plumbing fixtures in my favorite shopping spot, the local hardware store, comfortable in the realm of man talk.

In early snapshots there I stand in everlasting black and white, quietly at Dad's side in front of the stark, unlandscaped new house on Cottonwood Drive with its brand new Rancho Marjo house sign, or out on the patio next to the metal beds we slept in on balmy summer nights, my hand tugging lightly on his hip pocket, his hand on my shoulder, both of us with the same stance, one foot crossed casually over the other.

In my mind's full-color photograph, with its camera of infinite recordings, there I am with Dad. Picking out the Christmas tree year after year, listening to the banter of the Lion's Club members who warm themselves around the metal trash can bonfire, Dad's friendly blue eyes sparkling, his gapped front teeth glistening with easy smiles and laughter amid the camaraderie and accompanying bullshit being shoveled out in matter-of-fact man–style.

Patient, quiet, ever the observer, I tagged along with Dad in those early days over to Tommy's Liquor Store at the Adobe Road intersection known as Four Corners to get some milk, a 48-

cent purchase, that always left 2 cents change for a Tootsie Roll Pop or Double Bubble.

On hands and knees I watched Dad's multi-skilled hands trowel thick black mastic in sweeping circles onto the new convent floors, our voices hushed in the private, mysterious sanctuary of the nuns, my small hands mimicking his able hands as he laid each square of linoleum into its perpendicular pattern.

Hunkered down with Dad in the large drafty storage barn at the Doblers, he wrenched away on the orange and white Foremost Dairy trucks, the vocabulary of the refrigeration mechanic weaving its way into my memory bank like the mysterious green Freon gas re-circulating in its curious web of tubes and coils, compressors and the rhythmically whirring condenser fan.

When his work was done, the Doblers welcomed us into their loud, boisterous kitchen, offering all-you-can-eat bowls of ice cream scooped from huge cardboard containers with the generosity of spirit that the Dobler family circle embodied.

Every week Mom typed the Church bulletin onto long sheets of blue waxy stencil paper, handing the finished product over to Dad and me to run off on the clickety-clacking mimeograph machine in the rectory garage. Together we pushed the stencil tightly onto the drum, locking it into place with silver clamps, then collecting the damp inky sheets as they slipped into the catch basket.

I went along with Dad to Ben and Dick Bailey's Barbershop, reading Sports Afield magazines and listening to the father-son team's back and forth dialog. Later in my teens they nicknamed me "Crash," teasing me for "driving illegally" in my bare feet, as I chauffeured Dad to his hair cut when he was teaching me how to drive the big metallic silver Chevy Impala.

During my college summers, I worked a seasonal secretarial job on board the Base in the Public Works Office that adjoined the Facility Maintenance Building where Dad's office was. So we rode together to work in the early morning and quit work at the same time as the rest of the civil servants when the buzzer went off at 4:30 in the afternoon.

Dad liked to stroll down the hall for a visit during the day so he could chat with Pete Peterson, the chief engineer, and talk over Pete's personal fallout shelter designs, or rub elbows with the surveyors and draftsmen, who shared the same office space as my desk, where I spent almost the entire summer grappling with giant sheets of stiff paper, as I typed up the description, location and assigned number of every single building, shed or physical improvement on the entire Base.

Dad really preferred the atmosphere of Public Works, because it was under the command of the Navy, the branch of service he served with during WWII. He referred to his own boss at the time as "High Pockets," a disparaging term that quite graphically described the way this particular major strutted through the building. Dad had been around long enough to know probably too much; how the military establishment works, the waste, the short-sighted vision of each successive new kingdom and the temporary nature of the commitment to the civilians who were there year-in, year-out.

Dad laughed easily about it all, but he was under a lot of stress, and one day after lunch he came to my desk looking gray and worn and announced that he'd gone to the hospital earlier in the day and they thought he might have had a small heart attack, a condition that later would see him retiring earlier than he'd planned...

It is Christmas time, 1964. I am no longer a small child, but, no matter, I am still Dad's little girl, the one who goes along with him that dark winter night. We wend our way east of town, holiday lights twinkling from the scattering of cabins that dot the desert in what has since become known as Wonder Valley, through the ever-enchanting Sheep Hole Pass that curves upward and down, down, down into the low lands of Leslie saltworks, glistening like powdery white snow in the wash of our headlights.

Further into the Mojave we venture, turning onto the sparsely travelled Kelso Road, bewitched by shadows of roadside yucca spears and skittering mice that bolt across the road on their nocturnal errands.

Beyond the vast expanse of the sand dunes we round a curve, and suddenly, out of the darkness, the sparkling lights of the Kelso Train Depot beckon, dazzling as a white castle, a jewel in the midst of wilderness. Dad, who always seems to know everyone, is greeted like an old friend by the man behind the counter of the café, where tables are draped with white cloths as if expecting us. We have pie and then Dad shows me around, up a wooden staircase to the upstairs rooms and out to the shacks where the railroad workers live.

We put our ears to the rails, "like the Indians do, to tell when the train is coming," Dad tells me. And, sure, enough, soon the light of the engine beams in the distance, a mail bag is flung from a car as the train comes to a halt, and a couple of passengers step out onto the landing, as the train quickly speeds on its way and out of sight in the depths of the dark desertscape.

Mom and Dad hug, as Patsy, my beloved sister, shy as a filly, presents us with her new baby, Marlina Christine. Margot, mom. Lina, aunt. Christine, sister.

Christmas package, special delivery.

Patsy has come home to 29 Palms. Her husband Karren will follow shortly from Salt Lake City with their belongings.

This trip in the night to the Kelso Station really marks the end of childhood for both Patsy and me. Motherhood and the self-absorption of teenager-hood blur the connection between us for a time. But always we are two sisters, true blue playmates, two girls wrapped soulfully together, a bond secured by memories shared.

And Dad. Now Grampa. Now part of the wonder of starscape that beams down on us all. Dad's love as perpetual as desert sunshine, the true spirit of Christmas.

A Love Poem to My Sister
May 13, 1993

I love to rake.
It's a simple statement, but it bound us together, closer than the carefully chosen words of a love sonnet.
In Aunt Lina's yard, we took up our rakes. Long neglected, the entryway sand was uneven and weedy. I stooped to pull the dried grasses from the porch steps, while you pulled the leafy litter under the trees into tidy piles.
As I filled the dog's damp, cool bedding holes with sand, I scorned you for making so many piles that would have to be scooped up later into the wheelbarrow.
You just laughed and raked more leaves into piles.
We etched a neatly scratched design into the sand with our rakes, humming inwardly to ourselves, in unison.
I trimmed the dead overhanging branches of the palo verde, the rhythmical music of your rake in the background.
We turned on the hose to spray the earth and settle the dust, filling the air with childhood scents of wet desert soil and mesquite, creosote bush and oleander.
I love to rake, you said simply.
So do I, I answered.

April 17, 1993
7:45 a.m.

The power has gone out.
Uncle Pat.
This figure who has influenced our lives so deeply, whose approval we sought, who made us laugh, weep, rage, and who made us think. Whom we catered to, tiptoed around, avoided. One who could give and take in the same gesture. Who broke my heart with his unspeakable belittling of Dad. Who taught me how to put up my wall to defend myself from hurt and humiliation. Who knew so much and told such great stories, lost now.

Who is this person, so powerful? Even in the weakness of his deathbed, hardly able to speak, even the silence held a force.

Memories twinged with pain. Childhood laughter creeping in through the cracks. Trips in the trailer. Yosemite. Yellowstone. Inner tubes on the Merced. Brown bears in trash cans, sitting on the picnic table in the filtered forest morning light. Lina's light of love shining through.

Laughter and fear rolled into one. Uncle's rage. Laughter and fear rolled into one. Gaiety and rage. Loving gestures and biting words.

This powerhouse of a man. The power now out. Like dismantling a nuclear reactor. The generator is off, but the residual nuclear waste remains ... in each of us. Siblings and mother. Where to store it?

We'll stand at the monument, the tombstone with its graveside message written in Latin or Gaelic, some foreign language, whose meaning we will continue to quiz ourselves for. For there was always a test. "You should know the answer. You have a degree from the University of California, after all."

Uncle, with his 8th grade education, self-taught. A reader of encyclopedias. Knowledge of ancient history, sailing ships, the lumberjack industry, the Federal Reserve, mythology, the Jews, the tri-lateralists, geology, the Celts, the constellations.

A retired Captain in the Customs Service. The irony of serving in almost every branch of the Armed Services, even the calvary, and never fighting in a foreign war, waging his own conflicts on the home front. Arguments. Dad bristling. All worked up. Accusations. And Dad, Dad always reconciling. Inviting Uncle along on family picnics, for family dinners. Going up to Uncle's house at all hours to repair things or relocate some "lost" item. Dad's reservoir of tenderness in spite of all the barbs.

And I continue to probe for the loving memories, to balance the painful ones. To pull down the wall and let the feelings flow freely and honestly. Misty Moo Moo, my beloved pooch that Uncle and Lina got for me from the Hollywood Hills dog pound. Athena, Patsy's spirited horse, and Hector, my colt, my "Telstar," given and taken away. Lina, beloved Lina. Muriel and Herb, old dear friends from Wilmington. Crossword puzzles from the L.A. Times and hands of Canasta. Oil paint. Colorful language, archaic expressions. Knot tying. The Matson Lines. Rex the prospector at Old Dale Mine. Fosters Freeze ice cream cones for us and our dogs. Oats and molasses. Lanolin brushed lovingly into our hair. Patsy. Oh, Patsy and Uncle! What a long story in itself. She got all the goodies. And how grateful I am that she received his love and affection, to carry the good times forward, to preserve in loving memory.

Uncle Pat. The power is out. The energy remains.

The Glorious Years

After Uncle died, Patsy dedicated herself to cleaning, sorting and tidying up his place up in the Hansen Tract. The rest of us returned to our children and jobs right away, but Patsy stayed on after the funeral to help Mom with the paper details that swamp you at a time when the personal loss is overwhelming enough.

Every morning Patsy bicycled up the hill and set herself to sweeping, scouring and tossing out the trash and debris that had accumulated during the months of Uncle's absence when his health declined.

When I phoned to see how things were going, Mom would say, "I'm a little concerned about Patsy. She has this obsession with Uncle's house. I hope it isn't a mental thing."

"Just let her work. It's her way of grieving and letting go. It's something she has to do by herself," I said.

I knew what she was up to. Reliving the glorious years of Uncle Pat and Aunt Lina, as only we two could remember. Recalling the good times we had shared as a foursome. Hearing Uncle's voice of wisdom and wit, following him around in his workshop as he painted signs or oiled the garden tools. Feeling the warmth of Lina's soft bosom, holding on to her "big, ugly hands," as she called the hands that nurtured, toiled, beat mashed potatoes to a perfect whipped white smoothness, giving hands that comforted us with a love never held back.

The glorious years were highlighted by trips to Yosemite in the house trailer. Yosemite, where black bears swayed against each other like drunken sailors on the picnic table in our campsite, where we spent hours inner-tubing on the Merced River and Patsy protected me from a group of bullying boys with her fists, in the boxing style Uncle had taught her, and where we hooked in trout from the shore with squirmy, slimy red worms for bait. In the darkness we gathered in a circle of other Yosemite-enchanted campers to wait, hushed, for the Fire Fall, a cascading bonfire tumbling from the granite peaks far above us. Then later, in our communal dreams, we swooned to the lingering, haunting song of the Indian Love Call. "You'll belong to me. I'll belong to you-ooo-ooo-ooo-ooo-ooo-ooo."

    Now a dusty cardboard box in the tack room held the only remains of the things that used to be stored in the trailer. Sorting through that box meant tasting the Sugar Pops breakfast cereal poured into the colorful plastic newness of Melmac bowls. Breathing in the delicious smoky, sulphuric smell of the gas stove burners being lit by stout wooden matches at mealtimes. Shuffling the decks of cards and dealing out unwieldy large hands for endless hours of Canasta games. Red threes, Jokers, deuces, wildcards and naturals.

    Remember the time Uncle backed the trailer into the parking meter in the scorching summer heat of downtown Fresno? Did we dare laugh? When he spit out the truck window when the window was rolled up, did we dare laugh? When he got his jeans pocket stuck on the kitchen drawer handle in the trailer, and in a rage, he ripped his jeans right off, did we dare laugh?

    At night the dining table in the trailer converted into the bed that Patsy and I shared. She always got to sleep on the outside, which meant that, in spite of Uncle's meticulous reading of the level to keep one end of the trailer from being higher than the other, I rolled down hill in my sleep, to awake with an imprint of the window ledge on my face.

    Our last trip in the trailer took us to the Yellowstone, where we witnessed the forceful spouting of Old Faithful and the frothing, putrid-smelling flows of the sulphur hot springs that bubbled up from the inner earth like a powerful witch's brew. Bison and elk grazed in grassy meadows and the land sprang forth before us in endless majesty with mountains of forests, green and dark. Peace and power united.

    Four year-old Mark came along, his first and only trailer trip during those glory years with Lina and Pat. This trip stands as a marker event in my memories, for it was during these travels that Patsy experienced her last life-threatening asthma attack at age fourteen. After traveling across Northern California through the big timber country, weaving down treacherous windy roads, cautiously following or being nerve-wrackenly tailed by heavily laden, brake-grinding lumber trucks, we arrived in Arcata, where Uncle's step-dad, known to us as Uncle Tom, lived in a tiny hillside cabin. The man himself I hardly remember, but Uncle Tom's wooden leg, wrapped in smooth form-fitting saddle brown leather that laced up the front held great intrigue.

    The lumber mills belched out volumes of dark smoke from towering rusty stacks that stood like giant Bunsen burners next to the mill ponds. In the dark waters lay thousands of slain heaven-tickling giants, now lifeless piles of logs. Whether it was the smoke from the lumber mills or the sulphuric gasses of the Yellowstone, all I know is Patsy lay weak and wheezing on her bed in the darkness. Once again I sat at her side and watched her ribcage rise and fall, the exertion of each breath whitening her face, so that each freckle stood out on her weary face like a call for help. A doctor was summoned, who gave her an injection, and we were soon hustling home, out of the foggy seaside dampness, back to the sanctuary of the desert...

    Patsy is sitting on the back stoop of Uncle's house. The woodpile, dried by the sun to a powdery grey, is stacked tidily next to the cement steps. A weathered wooden box with oval handles and rusty metal strips tacked to the sides holds the kindling. The sand driveway is gated with a low chain link fence that requires Houdini-moves to fasten or unlock, moves that Patsy has mastered, but still leave me bewildered. The small house on the corner of Twilight and Saladin is a squatty '30s style California bungalow of white plaster with a red tile roof, raised foundation and wood floors covered over with an array of mis-matched colored carpets of mauve and orange displaying Uncle's bizarre sense of color.

    Walking out to the driveway Patsy laughs as she recalls the time I won that dang-blasted rooster at the Church Bazaar. To prove his roosterhood, the little chick soon started crowing and eventually crowed his way completely out of the neighborhood, when Mrs. Marvin up the street complained about the Spangenbergs having "barnyard animals" in a residential zone! When we overheard talk of getting rid of him, Patsy and I carried the rooster up the hill to Uncle's and created a home for him in a cage on the back porch to save him from the stew. Boy were Lina and Pat surprised on their next weekend visit when the rooster startled them awake with a morning serenade! To this day I suffer from "fear of poultry" due to this terrifying prize rooster, who chased me and Patsy's friend Maureen unmercifully around Uncle's yard until we were screaming bloody murder!

Now Uncle's dog Lady is smiling her contented dog smile, tongue lolling, soft brown eyes possessively watching Patsy's every move. My sister, tanned and fit, looks over "her" yard, quite at home here with Uncle's shy black and tan dog at her side. And I know she is thinking of all those times we have walked up hill to this old house, that long trek up Utah Trail to practice piano, to water the trees, to build the horse corrals, digging endless deep narrow holes for creosote-soaked fence posts, hoisting the corrugated asbestos roof pieces that shelter the stall. All those glorious memories.

Patsy has a vision and that vision won't let go. She is living in this little desert house. In 29 Palms, "the only place I ever feel calm."

Teenage Landscapes

From the kitchen door I watch you,
up on the neighbor's roof
with tools.
Tall, blonde, wiry, freckled.
There you are,
leaning against the lockers
alone at the curb, waiting for your bus.
A new boy in town.
Looking like he needs a friend.

On the dashboard of Aunt Inez's pocked-blue Ford station wagon
I prop my feet,
socks absorbing the scanty heat filtering through the vents.
The rear window, wide open, fills the car with icy blasts.
Our first "date,"
going to the snow.

Mom insists we first attend "Holy Class,"
and you comply,
coming along to Mrs. Fabian's high school catechism group.
A choice,
to be with me.

With gently falling snow powdering the windshield,
we peer together into the night
through ghost-like imagery of Joshua tree-and-yucca people
draped in their veils of white.

You are quiet
and strong
and we are shyly scared of each other.
Do we sense
in that night of dream-like panoramas,
that we are going to travel a long way together?
There is no need to rush?

You tell the simple truth,

no drama in the story.
That's just the way things are.
Your father's death in February,
heart attack, emphesema,
and your mother's death,
in summer,
breast cancer.
Age 15.
Both parents gone.
Uncle Jim and Aunt Inez,
your choice for home.

Into the snowy night we drive,
past granite boulders of my youth.
Split Rock, Skull Rock,
Jumbo Rocks.
Hidden Valley.
Twisting and turning our stories together,
as we circle into town.
I absorb the all of you.
Weathered leather jacket with sheepskin lining,
long lean legs in Levis,
Work boots and white t-shirt.
Inner landscapes shivering,
as elbows touch in your red Chevy pick-up,
with rounded hood and unreliable engine.
Motorcycle rides up the iron ore-strewn mountain
where the microwave tower blinks its red eye.
Pistol shooting in mesquite washes,
quail and dove whirring from the brush.
Hikes up Deep Creek in Hesperia,
before the dam stops the flow
to your childhood fishing hole.
Pulling off Hwy. 10, where wild hot winds funnel
through San Gorgonio Pass,
we wade and splash, clothes and all, to cool off
in the rushing clear rapids of White Water.

Spaghetti westerns and James Bond
on big white screens,
speakers wailing, propped on open windows.

Bodies sweaty in the heat of summer nights.
Tentative first kisses
in your aunt's worn green armchair,
moving on to body hugs
on bunk beds in your garage-room.
Scorpions parade in lamplight,
tails curving stiffly over armored backs,
while we talk.
Secretive midnight swims with Kathy and Ron,
in that old man's pool way down Adobe Road,
overhung with salty tamarisk trees,
bare limbs luring,
iridescent yellow-green by pool light,
mermaids and the gods.

In the gravel pit we park,
giant machinery casting monstrous, eerie shadows
against mountains of sand piles and crushed rock,
or on boulder-rimmed sandy roads,
we perch,
under deep night skies that curve over us,
leading us into unexplored landscapes.
Necking, nipples, lips,
red boxer shorts.
Waiting. Longing. Waiting.
Waiting for the word, Go.

The Coyote Chorus

Lying in the darkness of my bedroom,
I listen to the voice of the coyote.
Yip. Yip. Yip. Yippioooooo.
The high voices ring from the washes.
Hysterical, giddy voices
that make me feel giggly,
tickled to weakness in my belly.

Living on the fringe,
my coyote friends are shy but cocky,
wary yet bold, playful yet practical.
They sing.

I close my eyes and smile
as I see them singing,
lifting their slender snouts skyward
in a love-of-life chorus.
It is a lusty ballad of companionship, freedom,
grief and survival.
It starts spontaneously as a sudden cool breeze,
and builds into a wild crescendo of abandon.

The voice of the coyote lingers
long after the last note fades away,
long after the pack moves along
on its furtive night-time maneuvers.

Their voices stay with me through the years,
bursting from deep within
as I retreat into the darkness
to flee the heavy burdens inside my home.
On my driveway, under the black boundless sky,
I raise my snout and pierce the night
with my own wailing coyote voice.
The howling releases me,
freeing me from the loss
that pins me to my mattress
like the weight of a stone between my shoulder blades.

*For one heady moment I am free
from the reality behind the door.*

*In one swift twist of time,
a tree fells my mate,
paralyzing him,
altering the course of life as we thought we knew it,
leaving us momentarily off balance
and unsure of our future.*

*I close my eyes and howl,
yipping my silly sorrowful song,
so I too can move along on the forays of my fate,
scared but cocky,
weakened but boldly strong,
a giddy survivor
who knows the voice of the coyote.*

The Child's Question
Can I Be With You?

On Friday nights Patsy and I walked to the Starlite Drive-in Theater to roller skate. It was an outdoor rink with a concrete floor interlaced with many challenging cracks and fissures. Under a canopy of deep desert starscape we'd circle the rink, keeping rhythm to the scratchy music being drowned out by the scraping of metal-wheeled skates on cement.

When the records stopped playing, you could lean on the railing and watch the show playing on the southern screen and strain your ears to hear the muffled mumblings of Elvis or the bizarre screeching of the science fiction monsters that my sister loved so well.

Patsy's boyfriends would pay me a quarter to skate away and leave them alone to flirt and smooch. And soon I too was skating with the boy of my choice, Arthur, the boy down the road with the funny tip-toe walk and shiny dark brown hair that flopped into big teasing blue eyes. Round-and-round the rink we flew as fast as twelve year-old calves can muscle, racing and tugging each other, sweaty hands gripped together. *A marvelous dance across rough ground.*

Out of nowhere one of Patsy's Marine friends smacked into me. Hands behind his back, speed skater style, he'd lost control and knocked me down. I reached out to brace myself and fell with full weight on my wrist. Crumpled though I was, I got up and grabbed Arthur's nervous hand, blinking past the pain to skate on beneath the starlight. Not until I stopped skating did I realize I could not use my fingers and was unable to untie my skates.

Young bones heal quickly and I didn't give my broken wrist much thought until another night framed by starscape many years later...

I propped my son's casts on sculptures of pillows and held his swollen fingers in my hands. The evening sky's dance of stars slid in slow progression from east to west, as I read Kipling's stories of the great grey green Limpopo River and how the leopard got his spots.

In pain from severely fractured wrists, sleep did not come to my man-child.

I willed his deadened fingertips to feel, felt the throbbing in his crippled wrists, willed him to sleep through comforting childhood stories as I sat beside him.

"How do people have faith in God?" he suddenly asked, as the clock tipped despairingly toward 4 a.m. and visions of dislocated hands, flopping loose from their arm-bone anchors, raged behind his tensely closed eyelids.

Trying hard to breathe through the tightness in my chest, I whispered my answer into the darkness.

"All I can do is be with you."

It was a marvelous dance across rough ground.
The sunlight played along our pathway,
dappling the days with leafy shadow
and alternate splashes of blinding rays.
I fed my son pieces of sandwich,
tipped the straw so he could take a sip of soda,
took a bite of my own lunch,
while local building contractors and gallery owners
watched us, curiously,
from their tables outside the country store.

With both wrists bound in mummy-like casts,
up to his bent elbows,
all I could do was be here for him.
"Too much pain," he'd laugh
raising his casts above his head
in the shower.
I saw the tears
he tried to wash away with the bath water,
pins in his wrists pressing pain
against the walls of plaster casts.

This is the dance I've known.
Our four-some,
skating along under starlit skies,
holding hands together
as we clatter over the pavement of our days...

The earth is my home.
Brushstrokes of golden oak-studded chaparral,
wild mustard and purple globes of thistle,
torches of yucca on serpentine soil,
and the foundational textures of the Mojave Desert
grace my inner landscape.
Pacific tides pulled by perpetual lunar presence
have washed the shores of memory
since birth on the edge of the continent.

*But I have come to know the stars
in solitary midnight wanderings,
and through my son's bedroom window,
I see the faith of our fathers
in the dance of starlight
across the smooth landscape of dark space,
and watch a new constellation rising,
there,
in the dawn of morning,
the Sister of Mercy.*

Earth Musings

When a loved one dies, the laughter seems to ebb out of your heart, like a one-directional tide pulled by a waning moon that does not rise. At our family gatherings Dad's humor was darkly missing. That goofy smile that would come over his face, his way of coming up and nudging you with his elbow to share some witticism of the moment, the pleasure he got in giving you some simple practical gift, like a turkey baster or cuphooks that you'd idly mentioned you needed for your pantry shelf. And his homemade vocabulary with the hint of Germanic influence, words like Gefunga-dinga (a bad flu virus), Stoopnagle (idiot), Peeunger (penis), Pajumble (port-a-potty), Misgebote (brat), Buxtehude (the boondocks).

With his absence, I realized what a touchstone for acceptance and playfulness Dad had always been for me. A goofiness to balance the more serious, achievement-oriented self.

I have always felt singular. An observer, not particularly in step with the pace of others. The remoteness of my childhood desert upbringing had kept me insulated from the cultural changes of the '50s and '60s. Even movies shown at the local theaters were often a couple of years old. Radio stations didn't boom their frequencies out that far, except after sundown, when Wolfman Jack from Mexico or K-O-M-A, Oklahoma City, raised their megawatts of power to bring us the Top Ten. I had no idea our tucked-up skirts were "minis," our midriff blouses or go-aheads part of a fashion trend. I was just who I was with no extraneous social definition, a desert life form, as individuated as the Joshua tree or beavertail cactus to its unique ecological niche.

Now the mourning that clouded my spirit exposed an unexpressed passion, brooding in me, wanting release, yet not knowing where to land. I could walk off the sadness, but I could not shrug off the restlessness. One January day I resigned from the busy-ness of my long-term job as publicist, programmer of workshops and accounting for the local arts association I had helped launch with Connie, my working partner and friend of many years. "It feels like a divorce," she cried.

But, one never severs the ties with ones you have walked with in the spirit of love. You carry them forever in every beat of your heart. I needed to take this step, set my own pace, reconnect with my own voice.

The loss of Dad nudged me to sit down and write these collected memories of growing up on the desert, as a prayer of gratitude for all he meant to me.

"Earth Musings" is a sampling of my emerging voice as a writer, which found an outlet for expression during a five-year stint as editor of the Santa Ynez Valley Women's Environmental Watch newsletter. This position provided me with the unexpected gift of an audience for my internal landscape of wonderings.

When I was a young girl, I often heard my mother chastising her older sister, "You're hiding away, Lina. Tucked away up here in your house. You need to get out more."

My aunt would look at her with a confused expression and reply, "I'm perfectly happy, Margot. I love sitting in my garden under the pine tree, tending the plants and my lemon tree, listening to the birds. This is what I like to do."

To my mother, the Capricorn achiever, this type of life was incomprehensible. How could her sister be content "just" being at home in her yard without an identity "out in the world?"

My childless aunt was equally baffled by her sister's criticism. "She's raised five beautiful children," she once said to me. "Is she not satisfied? And why is she picking on me and my choice?"

Their conversation has become my internal conversation. It comes to me in their own voices in the morning, as I bend to pull out the grasses and weeds along my garden path. As I pull and pitch the weeds onto the compost heap, I feel an inner wordless bliss. I can hear humming, a song from my ancestors' past. Peasant women tending the vegetables, working in the soil as I am now. The humming is as real as the dirt under my fingernails, these sisters of the past, singing as they work, the cool breezes waving the grasses, the sun on their broad backs, smiles at their lips. Sisters in the soil.

And then the other voices, those of the sisters, Margot and Lina, interrupt the humming. Their conversation, my own voices within my head, a back-and-forth tug o' war as I try to realize my Self, struggling with the feeling that I must somehow justify my choice to be at home now, without my work-world identity. What significance can my puttering have in this fast-paced, achievement-oriented, consumer culture of ours? Where does my weed-pulling, pond digging, herb planting, bird listening, sky watching, cloud chasing, earth scratching fit in the '90s?

I choose to luxuriate in the moments of simple bliss and leave the voices to the past. Let the humming of the soil sisters fill my ears as I hoe and plant and "idle" in my garden!

Los Olivos Meadows

The land used to flow. Undulating hills of native oat grasses, lupine, owl's clover, mariposa lilies, Chinese lanterns. All waving their splendor of colors.

The land told you where to walk, following the roll of the soil, picking your steps through the grasses, taking the trail of the deer's path. Grey-green sagebrush on the scruffy, windswept slopes to the west and south, the arid section, flanked by the rolling oak tree canyons, lush with miner's lettuce and those abundant deep blue flowers clumped in the shade of the oaks. Fiesta flowers to pick and stick against your chest like a beautiful badge.

My feet seemed to know the way, making an unprescribed pathway up hill and down, following the ridge lines, bounding carelessly down the grassy slopes to the flatland.

Now a dusty slash of white road dictates where I go, the soil a fine deep powder, unfamiliar, not at all what I thought the land beneath was made of. You sink to your ankles in the powdery stuff, laid bare naked by the graders.

The land has been cut, wounded by man's desire to dominate and settle. A colony of deep purple lupine stands in contrast to the gouged earth, where a deep trench houses the foreign cement pipes that will soon bring water and power to the buildings that will scar this landscape.

The quail still call and the sounds of insects almost drown out the traffic from the highway below, if you'll allow it. The dry oat grasses make their own brittle tunes in the breeze, and Elsie, my companion dog, crashes through the brush, interrupting the music of the grasses.

I love it up here, my personal musing spot. The land still speaks to me while it can. And so I come here. As often as I can.

"The Peace of Wild Things"

When despair for the world grows in me
and I wake in the night at the least sound
in fear of what my life and my children's lives may be,
I go and lie down where the wood drake
rests in his beauty on the water,
and the great heron feeds.
I come into the peace of wild things
who do not tax their lives with forethought
of grief. I come into the presence of still water.
And I feel above me the day-blind stars
waiting with their light. For a time
I rest in the grace of the world, and am free.
—Wendell Berry

In May I had the pleasure of attending a reading by Wendell Berry at UCSB. What a gentle, softly spoken powerhouse! In a question-and-answer session the audience seemed to be grasping for a guru who has the answers for everything, from how to combat pessimism, to what to include in the school curriculum, and even whether or not to buy bottled water. I quickly scribbled down notes, hoping to save Wendell Berry's many quotable words of humor and unpretentious wisdom. So much of what he said struck a chord with the awareness that Women's Environmental Watch hopes to generate.

An apostle of local food marketing economics, Berry is currently devoting most of his time to a pilot program in rural Kentucky. The goal of his project is to give the local people a chance to do something themselves that's good, that they can control and be hopeful about, a farming project that maintains and sustains the connectedness between eaters and producers. With local food marketing the consumer gets better, fresher food that isn't being grown and engineered for transport, plus the folks get a chance to have some influence.

Do a small thing, he advises, so as not to get lost in the abstraction of a movement. Take charge of the small things. Be subversive, take responsibility for your personal economy.

We can't worry about the future or we'll get sucked down a hole. Our time is now. To avoid sinking into pessimism, we must go beyond vision. Having a vision isn't enough, Berry says. Hope comes from work and action. Gather examples of things that work.

I especially appreciated Berry's comments on what he considers to be "the great arts," the arts of domestic affection, child-rearing, neighborliness and farming as the fundamental art.

From his book, "The Farm," which he referred to as an operator's handbook, Berry's words told of the rhythmic, repeated cycles of farming, the seasons' work, a gentle way to farm and work the land, where diversity increases the yield.

Go by the narrow road, forget the paved road. Make yourself a place for love to reach the ground, kindly working love.

Be thankful. Work done in gratitude is prayer. Learn to live with neighbors never chosen, as well as those you've chosen.

The law of the neighborhood is "Never buy far off what you can buy at home."

The land must have its Sabbath for rest and enrichment, or take it when we starve.

Live like a tree. It doesn't grow beyond the power of its place.

And my favorite quote: "A cow's a good excuse to bring you home from places you don't want to be."

Morning Musings at the Shore of Lake Cachuma

At water's edge, the human race took form.
On the banks of rivers, civilizations began. And flourished.
Muddy and polluted, crystal clear and free-flowing,
stagnant and brackish,
at water's edge we stoop for life.
There is no other option but Water.

The sunlight glistening on the water pulsates on my closed eyelids. I am not fully awake yet, although I'm dressed, have eaten breakfast, and have ridden along the fifteen miles to Lake Cachuma.

Tim is fishing from the dock, and I sit, mesmerized by the mist rising off the water. Slowly I come into consciousness. A half dozen loons keep me entertained. They dive and splash just below the surface of the water, then squawk in triumph, their long thin beaks holding up a minnow to show off to their friends before gulping it down and diving again.

As the sun rises higher, the water turns a deep forest green at water's edge where the oak trees grow, a sparkling blue-green where it ripples in the center of the cove.

The restlessness I awoke with fades away with the evaporating mist. I breathe with the rhythm of the lapping water, releasing anxiousness to the soft, gentle waves, losing myself in the rusts, golds and greens on the sloping hillside across the opposite shore.

The loons continue to play. They seem to dive on cue with an unspoken language. Now close together, now spread far apart, scouting the waters in a long straight line, coming back together in a tight group. Each time one is successful at catching a fish, he squawks a message, "I've got one!" to the others. Now they move away onto the open water, out of my sight.

The water laps. Tim casts. Ducks preen on the rocks in the sunshine, revealing violet pin feathers. Commuters, shoppers and sightseers push on through up Hwy. 154. The water laps...

As often as I've been to Lake Cachuma, it always awes me how much more I experience the essence of this rare beauty of a place when enhanced by naturalist Neal Taylor's trained eyes and well-versed observations.

The January W.E. Watch boat trip was my third time to be guided on a lake tour narrated by Neal. Having fished the area for steelhead with his father and Zane Grey, even before the lake existed, before the dam, Neal knows this place. His eyes don't miss a twitch of a deer's ear behind the brush, or the "friendly approach" of the courting red-tailed hawk dragging its talons, or the "pages of free history" written in the compressed fossilized marine life in the shoreline rocks, or the 3-pound bass beneath our boat!

He tells us of this "Chumash people's paradise," how the native dwellers lived off the land, utilizing the yucca for soap, needle and thread and food, the tobacco tree for insect repellent, the grasses for baskets, and the Spanish moss for wound packs, diapers, and sleeping mats.

"Now we shop in convenience stores and don't understand our environment," he notes.

Ten ornithologists once spotted 276 varieties of birds in four hours at Cachuma. One year 75-80,000 geese over-wintered here. Today we spot Western grebe, Clarks grebe, osprey, great blue herons, turkey vultures, egrets, butcher birds, coots, mallards, belted kingfisher, cormorants air-drying their feathers with out-stretched wings, and the nests of bank swallows.

We don't witness the 90-inch wingspan of the condor on this outing, but we see a magnificent flock of Canadian geese and many gulls feeding in the lake's bays, gulls affectionately nicknamed "bagels."

Neal points out the north shore, closed to people to safeguard the land and watershed from fire, and to protect the people (and in turn the wildlife) from encounters with the bear, mountain lion, coastal mule deer, beaver, and nesting bald eagles who make their home here.

We skirt alongside Arrowhead Island where a herd of 20-25 deer live and see the log line in Santa Cruz basin, broken by the weight of debris during recent storms. Much of the debris had washed down since the Marre fire. The log line helps replenish fish life by providing habitat and protects nesting birds, at the same time preventing debris from clogging the lake.

The presence of banana slugs, Neal informs us, reveals that redwoods once grew here!

In closing, Neal shares his great pride in the Lake Cachuma facility. The tranquility is what gives the lake its unique characteristics. Fathers and sons can fish here peacefully, undisturbed by large power boats. From his point of view, the off-season is the best. Thousands of visitors enjoy this place. It is a free-enterprise park, he tells us, not tax dollar supported, that generates $20 million each year for the local economy.

River Reverie
June 1, 1995

A river runs through Buell-town.
Early morning I work my way through the war of the willows
to discovery.

A flannel-shirted man with ruddy face passes on the dusty path,
a pair of 12-inch trout dangling on a string,
snouts bloodied with their final battle.
"Breakfast," he tells me of the beauties. "Don't tell anyone
about my fishin' hole!"

Tall iris grow at waterside,
the plants standing aloof from one another,
yet united as a colony.
Clear waters stream through long green strands of moss hair.
Tadpoles lounge in still waters on the sandy bottom
like giant black sperm waiting for action.
At a bend white water splashes over boulders,
while swallows dance on invisible currents
choreographed by insects.

Traces of Marlboro Man jerk the senses.
Hound dog bounds away to chase a jack rabbit
along the dry rocky river bed.

A rank odor of dried moss and river mud
draws my eyes to the fishy smelling earth —
dry moss matted against stones like a maiden's hair
on pillows after sated passion.

The dog darts lackadaisically at red-tipped black birds.
I stand waist-deep in the clear, still waters
of my swimming hole.
I meander with deer tracks along the sandy bank,
my toes crunching in clods of dry clay bricks underfoot
that hint at summertime.

Stony grey freeway bridges stand sculpture-like against a
backdrop of foggy skies and oak-studded hillsides.

Swallow song speaks of peace.
Reverently I wend my way back through willows to the roadway,
while violent words—
Lightin' strikes twice
F---, Dare and Dark
Trade
Greenpeace sucks
splashed in red and blue on concrete walls—
ricochet on river rock.

August, 1995

    The other morning I stood on the runway at the Santa Ynez Airport and waved goodbye to my daughter, as she took off for an enviable adventure-filled trip to the wilds of Wyoming. As her plane banked and then disappeared in the river fog, the vagabond spirit in me was stirred, that wanderlust that makes one yearn for "greener pastures" and wilder places. The hermit in me who longs for solitude and anonymity, and who dreams of being surrounded by unspoiled native vegetation and wide-open vistas, was roaring to be heard. I wanted adventures. I wanted to escape, to get away from it all, you know what I'm sayin'?

    It has been the American way to "go west, young man," to seek out new territory and explore the wilderness. The desire to escape the confines of urbanization and all the problems that over-crowding brings, is motivating many Californians to "move out," to find quieter, less populated areas in which to raise families or retire. Of course, this mass migration only leads to the urbanization and "un-wilding" of the very wild places we have escaped to. We take all the trappings of our former selves with us, and then, ten years later or so, scorn all the others who have "followed us" there and find ourselves, once again, engaged in local environmental protection rallies, writing letters to the editor and attending city council meetings (or not), and planning commission hearings (or not), just like we did (or didn't) in our previous communities, and wondering what happened to the pristine surroundings we once knew and cherished and thought would always be there.

    Just last spring in my wanderings I stumbled across the Ranchitas Estates in San Luis Obispo County. Tucked behind Lake Lopez, 6400 acres of former ranch land was being subdivided into 40 large parcels and auctioned off.

    During the months of March and April I found myself returning again and again, taking possession of two pieces of land in particular that seemed to have my name on them. Picnicking far off the roads under the oaks in a beautiful meadow rimmed on three sides by rugged hillsides covered with blooming sage and myriads of wildflowers, I began to settle in. All this native landscape could be mine! I could roam the hills in solitude, my very own 60 acres with its majestic oaks and cypress, chaparral and grassland, seasonal waterfalls and creeks. Or I could stand at the top of the ridgeline and look out over the rest of the valley and watch the incoming storms and the moon rise, surrounded by the simple silence.

"Wild turkey, wild peacock, bobcat, coyote, fox and bear are all a part of the natural setting," the brochure boasted.

Around about my third trek back to sit on my land and imagine myself living there, my husband said simply, "I don't have to own this land to enjoy it." Hmmmm.

On a later trip, as we kayaked up the lagoon east of Lake Lopez, unusually full after the ample winter rains, he commented again, "I don't have to own this canyon to appreciate it and be filled with its beauty." Oh.

So, of course, realistic thinking started seeping in then, with questions to be answered, like, "What will this Ranchita landscape look like when the equestrian enthusiasts move in and mark their territory with Kentucky Bluegrass white fencing? Will I be able to see the neighbor's two-story Victorian monstrosity from my own small rustic meadow dwelling tucked privately beneath my circle of oaks? Who are these neighbors and will I fit in? Will they clear out all their surrounding native vegetation and replace it with lawns and plastic playground equipment? Will the coyote and deer still meander across my meadow once I'm all settled in? And, most importantly, what will I have gained in terms of a sense of community and connection? How many years will I have to live here before I feel truly at one with the sagebrush? When will I be able to sniff the wind and know I am home? Will I come to know this landscape so that I hold it inside my soul, inside my dreams and unspoken memory?

So now I find myself drawn to writings that speak to that sense of place. I listen to Terry Tempest Williams describe a "Home Stand Act," which would "inspire and initiate a community of vigilance and care toward the lands we inhabit." An act that "would give us courage to honor the stay option and dig in, set down roots."

"It may be that the most radical act we can commit is to stay home," Williams writes. "Otherwise, who will be there to chart the changes?"

Who will be there to cry for the losses or to notice when or if the birds return to their nesting grounds? Who else will testify that the owls' clover and lupines, once lush upon the Los Olivos Meadows, are not blooming anymore? Who will remain to tell the stories that originate in the land, the waters, the skies of our home?

To stay or to go?

"All of us, I think," Wendell Berry writes, "are in some manner torn between caring and not caring, staying and going." His philosophy contains two absolute laws. First, we can't exempt ourselves from living in this world as users, and second, we can't exempt ourselves from care. We must deal with the issues raised by our very essential need to "use the earth."

So, of course, I'm staying. I want to play a part in proving that we humans, right here in the Santa Ynez Valley, can "adapt our work and our pleasure to our place so as to live in it without destroying it."

We can't continue to play western frontiersman and hope to move on when we've used up our resources. We at home are the players who have to initiate the long-term caretaking of what we love about our landscape. So, we remain, vigilant, insisting that our government, local and federal, remain accountable. We become active members of our community to learn how to do this most effectively, in a spirit of partnership and mutual support.

January, 1996

All the Holiday socializing has left my hand mute.
Too much verbal stifling the imagery.
Blocking entry into the soul.
11:00 p.m. I walk in full moonlight.
On the streets of Los Olivos, no one stirs.
Creatures of habit, all indoors,
this spectacle of star-space lost to their awareness.

In the fullness of an angel hair strewn sky
in the crisp night air, with clear deep space
and those familiar far-away lanterns of Orion's Belt
beckoning and winking,
I walk in the full January moonlight,
and am reminded of why I am here.
In this Valley home.
To be part of the big sky again.
To feel embraced by the universe.

Owls hoot from darkened hillsides.
White bark of sycamore glistens.
Furry muffs of mistletoe entwine tree trunks.
In a huddle of dry grey sagebrush I sit,
letting my ragged edges be smoothed
by soft contours of the swelling earth.
Opening eyes wide to absorb shadow and skyscape.
Letting the silence speak.

What a loss, the greatness of this night,
wasted on humankind,
locked indoors exchanging wisdoms,
voices clanging against walls,
echoing and banging,
words against words,
against walls, against walls.
Wisdom empty of the depths of the silent night experience,
found only in solitary walks,
in the fullness of a January moon.
En-light-ened by the night.

March, 1996

Drywall dust powders my keyboard. The workers banter their private contractor language in the background—measuring, scraping, pounding, troweling, sawing, drilling. The kitchen walls have been stripped of the familiar accumulated funk. "Witches' weeds," as my sister calls my dried herbs and flowers, lie about the living room, draped on piles of dishes, foodstuff, and stacks of kitchen clutter removed from old cabinet drawers.

Amazing that I could create fairly decent menus from this odd array of cookware and mis-matched plates. What's odder yet is that I could probably get used to stepping over boxes of junk to find my spot on the couch where my books and magazines and notes lie strewn in haphazard piles on the floor. I'm learning about kitchen remodeling in quick-study fashion! I've been having a hard time finding my computer space, not to mention a mindful space, so, excuse me, that this newsletter is somewhat dusty and delayed.

During this election season, many of us have been involved in political campaigning for the candidates of our choice. This is my first really committed venture into politicking, and what seems most valuable to me, as I walk precincts, talk on the phone, put up signs, and attend meetings, is the connectedness we share as community members. Folks are generally receptive to a friendly neighbor. I've had some good laughs over the phone with complete strangers who seem like long-time acquaintances by the time we're done chatting. Some people haven't a clue about who's running for what and they appreciate any information they don't have to seek out by themselves. Others are "polar opposites" and we smile at each other and say, "As you wish," respecting our differences, for we have to remember that diversity is a healthy thing, in nature or in philosophy.

But a common link that I feel, whether going door to door or greeting people at the market, is our sense of "home" and belonging, a spirit of community that encourages being approachable to each other. We don't ever want to lose this connectedness. We're going to need each other in the 21st century more than ever before, and a friendly hello on the sidewalk lends itself to future cooperativeness.

When you look out your windows on a sunny morning, can't you almost hear a collective "aaah," as we acknowledge the good land we have chosen to live in? By embracing a sense of community and the ethics of cooperation, and acknowledging our connectedness to the natural world, I do believe we can create an era of empowerment and celebration, rather than an age of disabling anger and disenfranchisement.

May, 1996

Dear Mom,
I'm going to the weeds.
Love, Kate

  I recently found this note among my collection of mementos. It is my daughter's first "refrigerator note" to me. These are poignant times. Kate is about to graduate from high school, and when I look at her, I know I have done at least one grand thing, which is really enough success to claim in one lifetime. She has shown me so many inner and outer worlds that would have gone unexplored without her to guide me. (I know there are others of you out there who know just what I'm saying.)
  When I read this precious, crinkled little note, I know I have wordlessly passed on my love of the land to my daughter. Children know the earth. Kate found her place for solitude, play, replenishment and safety early on, in this naturally landscaped field just down the road where the old walnut barn once stood and the tall wild grasses, golden mustard, shady old trees and prickly thistles grow.
  These days, when Kate heads out in her bus to Grass Mountain "to read and write and wander," I'm proud of her for feeling free enough to go off on her own into a place of refuge, that fortunately for us Valley dwellers, still exists just up the road, or, if we're really lucky, just out our doorstep.
  I've been listening to a series of tapes from a nature writers' workshop held this past January in Florida. In a discussion of Literature and Advocacy, writer Joy Williams asks some thought-provoking questions. "Is nature receding from us? Is environmentalism becoming a meaningless word? Do we love our own kind enough to fight for our future, for our collective survival?"
  As we continue to carve out the role that Women's Environmental Watch can play in helping to preserve our local habitat for the health of our local humanity, we can always return to John Muir's leadership. Muir took people into the

wilderness where they could have fun and fall in love with the wild. "A simple strategy," writes David Brower in "Let the Mountains Talk, Let the Rivers Run."

When John Muir took Teddy Roosevelt camping in Yosemite, Roosevelt "went away rhapsodizing about natural cathedrals." He came to know personally that wildness could save him and save the country. Standing at the Grand Canyon's rim, Teddy could say, "Leave it as it is. The ages have been at work on it, and man can only mar it." David Brower has a further admonition that I like, "Don't ever give up what you haven't seen."

So, to return to our role in advocacy, I think we're on just the right track when we load up a group of assorted people—supervisors, commuters, Santa Barbarians, shop owners, children, laborers, movie stars, housewives, ranchers, teachers, newcomers—and treat them all to an early morning float on the jewel of Lake Cachuma; when we carpool up to Rancho El Roblar to learn about holistic resource management practices, by pressing our soles on the land we usually just view from our car windows; when we invite others to visit the Sedgwick and breathe in the oak woodlands, the wildflowers, the vernal pools, the rolling hills with all our senses.

Advocacy for environmental awareness starts best on the simple level of sharing—sharing what we know and what we treasure. No words are even necessary. These shared experiences help remove the "us vs. them" posturing, so that together we can stand on common ground and find solutions to the problems we have all collectively created.

A field of weeds down the road for a child's hide-away, a sagebrush-covered slope, a favorite overlook of the valley, three oak trees in a neighborhood pasture, a section of creek that meanders through town—each of our little Yosemites is worthy of reverence. Quietly and simply the love of the land is passed on, and what a gift—to connect someone you love to that which is in our human best interest so save.

Dear Kate,
I've gone to the weeds.
Love, Mom

July, 1996

*"When from our better selves we have too long
Been parted by the hurrying world, and droop,
Sick of its business, of its pleasures tired,
How gracious, how benign, is Solitude."*
— William Wordsworth

Today is a day of solo wanderings. Along the rural back roads of the county I listen to mellow tunes, daydream, sort out in my mind which newsletter items to cover this time around, and pat my big red hound as she lolls her tongue and rests her head in my lap, content to be on a ride-along with her human.

While my own car is in the shop, I've taken over my daughter's bus, which she affectionately calls "Honey." There's something inherently "vagabond-isch" about being behind the wheel of a '60s VW. Every little jaunt becomes an excursion. And you're part of this family of friendly folks, who smile and wave at you when you pass, give you the peace sign, and say, "Right on!"

So, I'm on the road, chasing clouds, taking detours, and definitely taking my time. Silently I find myself rejoicing in the variety of scenery that slips by as I meander, humming to the simple pleasurable sound of "my" VW bus engine's rhythmical "purr." On the way back from early morning business in Santa Maria, I toodle along Hwy. 135 and witness the abundance of our North County's farm crops and range land. Tractors move through the furrowed rows, crews of workers pick and hoe, and lean together, taking a break under shady trees. Miles of newly plowed fields staked into unnatural parallel lines and denuded rolling hillsides reveal the latest buy-up of ag land being devoted to the monoculture of vineyards, testimony, perhaps, to the consumer's increased thirst for wine and decreasing appetite for red meat on the hoof. This gives rise to several miles of reflection on what will happen to the diversity of plant life and pollinators (all those butterflies and bees, bats, flies, moths and birds, and host of microbial critters) once these hundreds and hundreds of acres are covered over with grapevines.

Here and there cattle dot the sage-covered hillsides. In my musing, I can't help but be grateful to the cattle rancher, for he is the tender of the open space we so long for and need for our communal health and well-being. I have to believe and trust that most ranchers are smart businessmen, who want to preserve the productivity of the land. We share the tainted title of "environmentalist," and must join hands to preserve the treasured lifestyle the rancher has enviously inherited, thus preserving the sacred and endangered treasures of our county's rural landscapes.

Summertime! The wanderlust is too strong. Once back home, I pack up a quick bag lunch, whistle for my pooch, grab my beach chair, and hit the road again!

Hwy. 246 through Buellton-west gives cause to more pensiveness. Houses are popping up in open fields, with a new dull-pinkish brick wall enclosing a suburban-style neighborhood, a wall just begging for some clone-town plantings to prevent a graffiti message or two. And there are now seven (soon to be eight) choices for pumping gas (a sure indicator of anticipated growth). Wake up, Buellton. Your neighborhood is a-changin'.

Hurry down the road!

Jalama Beach Road. One of my all-time favorites! Winding roads wend through bean fields, past farmhouses and old barns. Orchards of Queen Anne's lace, on the verge of bursting from green buds into delicate pompoms of white clusters, line the side of the road. The dried brown stalks and creamy flowers of dried thistles enhance the green background of dense tidy rows of peppers. Cattle graze on steep slopes. Hawks dance drunkenly on canyon thermals.

The road winds and winds, a second gear challenge for Honey. And suddenly, around the bend and over the railroad tracks, an expansive turquoise sea! The curve of the beach cliffs hugs me in a welcoming embrace.

Surfers go right for the power of the waves that curl and cross and beat the sand into smooth hard beaches, just perfect for planting my beach chair and towel. Elsie the dog lounges next to me, a friendly man offers me a crocheted flower he has made, mother and tots build a fortress of drip castles, shell gatherers stroll, sun worshipers bake, while I, in my mind, write this article...

Ah, summer! My season for indulging in the state of reverie, experiencing unity with the world without and the world within. Solitude. Such a valuable resource for the soul.

Well, I see thunderclouds ... Gotta go chase them!

Circles of Reverie

*A tumbleweed blows daintily by
and gentle sands
ripple and regroup
along sandstone cliffs,
peppering lips with salty grit,
mother earth's ribs
revealed in feminine ridges
laid naked by the winds.
Ice crystals form
a dotty sky,
spreading like a jeweled fan
in late afternoon sunshine.*

*Rewarded by solitude,
and wildness
the earth child-woman
lies against protruding cliffs,
and soon
she too will disappear
into beach landscape,
a sand-covered sculpture.
Lone woman on-the-rocks
looking seaward,
a sand goddess
blending into beach
into broken bits of shale
into strands of dried kelp
and bits of sea creature bone,
in solitude,
finding the quiet center
once again.*

*The tides speak to her
of ancient rhythms.
No need for answers,
just relish being.
Grateful for the sight
to behold sunlight
on white-capped waves
that lick the sandy shore
with frothy curls of pounding surf,
while drapes of infinite clouds
stretch across the land,
reaching out to an endless sea.*

*The earth child-woman
waits, watches and longs.*

The teenager woman.
Long blonde hair shining in the sun,
easy laughter sprinkled throughout her sentences.
Fit and trim, yet soft under gauze blouses.
Listening to loud music in her car.
I'm a dreamin' woman I guess that's my problem.
I can't tell when I'm, not bein' real."

Chatty. Easily blushing as she speaks of her own antics.
Simple wisdoms, spoken simply.
Self-expressions pouring out,
revealing how life has touched her.
Spontaneous.
Now.
"So easy to talk to. An air of easy self-confidence,
walking easy on the earth."
"I think you can do anything you decide to do,"
he says.

And,
though charmed so,
he saw through it.
The loneness. A sadness.
"Something you said. A fleeting look."
He saw it and spoke to it.
She, of course, shrugged it off,
and kept chattering.
What to do when so transparent?
Facing herself, in the eyes of the other.
Reflected back.
A lunar mirror.

A girl inside, now wanting to be revealed,
bubbles out in spontaneous giggles,
laughing at herself and her world.
A girl inside
who can't reach through the patterns.
Life so serious, too soon.
Learning to respond by working hard.
At everything.
Give her a task so she can do it.
Romantic dreamer, step aside.

Now, beyond busyness,
Realities slip through the cracks,
of her mask.
She's surprised it was obvious.
She'd thought no one could notice.
No facades,
without busy beads to fondle.
Exposed.

Find a direction to point to.
And go there. Do it.
Scared.
Every new step makes waves,
breaks the foundation with an awkward crack.
Truth.
Search for it.
Move. Make a move.
Now?
Keep quiet until sure of the truth?
When is that?
Now?
What is that?
Find it. Face it.
Now.

Walnuts fall,
breaking free from their husks as they hit the cement.
She grasps them tenderly in her fingers.
Surprisingly, even though the shell has cracked wide open,
so abruptly,
the fruit nourishes.
Dry. Meaty. Rich with ripened maturity.
Tasty to the tongue,
yet bitter, with experience,
creating an achiness on the acid-washed palate.
Cracked open.
Perfect symmetrical halves, sun-wrinkled,
lie in shattered pieces in her palm.

The second walnut she breaks open gently,
leaving halves intact.
The riches inside lie in their beds,
thin lifelines etched in pale sandalwood color,
weaving across the blonde dimpled curves of the nut.
Open gently so,
the partner in each separated half stays intact.
Not broken. Whole.
Sunlight streams inside.
The breeze whispers and soothes.
The truth is out.

The Broken Rose Bush

*The rose vine sprawls
broken and twisted,
forceful winds toppling her to the ground.
Entangled in the redwood trellis,
trapped by her very weight,
and years of wrapping and weaving
her gentle tendrils,
in and out, around and through
the heart of her support system.*

*The redwood arch now lies snapped,
broken into sections.
The weight of the whole
wrenching the roots from the soil.
They grasp and hold on,
pulling against the weight
of the tangled mass.*

*The broken rose bush.
Downed by stormy winds,
the branches cling,
strained and broken,
onto severed redwood forms,
no longer arching
in open welcome.*

*The man comes,
to free her.
With clippers held in strong fingers,
he snips the vines apart
to release the burden.
Letting her grow
new and fresh.
Letting the life force flow
into new vines,
stronger and freer than before.
Letting the released tendrils
wind as they will,
no structured archway*

*to guide or direct the growth,
but free
to twist and turn
and dance
in new directions.*

*Roots strong and intact,
nurtured from the soil of infancy.
Reaching to the sky,
draping along the waiting outstretched fence rails,
to bloom anew.
To be seen anew.
To bud
and open,
beautiful,
sweet-smelling,
fine,
and stronger than before.*

*The broken rose bush.
Split apart by forceful winds,
freed by gentle touch
into rebirth.*

Gyroscope: a wheel or disk mounted to spin rapidly about an axis and also free to rotate about one or both of two axes perpendicular to each other and to the axis of spin so that rotation of one of the two mutually perpendicular axes results from application of torque to the other when the wheel is spinning and so that the entire apparatus offers considerable opposition depending on the angular momentum to any torque that would change the direction of the axis of spin.

What? Could you repeat that please?

You speak of Jovial Junker days,
Mexico and Model-A's,
B-17's and Messerschmidts,
Cessna 140's and Stukas.
And two souls collide in mid-flight.
The horizon is steady.
Fly me to the landing zone.

It's the chuck that spins on the lathe.
Your voice, our touch.
I spin too.

I am free to spin, to laugh, to sway,
to roam alone, to toss my mane.
I'm president of the Brat Club, remember?

Words. With shared special meanings.
Knurling with x's and o's.
Disarmador. A screwdriver, you say.
My ears hear only disarm—
letting down my defenses,
to let you into my world.

A gyroworld of connecting language
and lunar laughter.
Words and gestures,
torque us into connection.

> *I spin, you spin.*
> *I breathe, you breathe.*
> *Indian death grips and butterfly touches.*
> *Talk about torque!*

*Interruptions change the direction of our chatter.
Opposition becomes a new shared direction.
Later we can always return to the pattern,
circle back to take-off.*

*I am the wheel spinning. I am the free one.
Free to rotate between two axes,
perpendicular to each other,
yet sharing the same air space.
It's some kind of wonderful.
It must be illegal or something.
I want us to go on forever.
In our gyroworld.*

I watched the butterfly dance.

Singly,
>*Tiptoeing on the velvet of the*
persimmon-colored petals,
daintily sipping the powdery treasure
hidden deep within the
yellow erectness of the flower's center.
Wings folding and unfolding.
In touch.
Nourished.

In doubles,
>*darting in a figure-8 dance,*
nuzzling in flight,
circling each other,
touching where the circles meet.

Green eyes into green eyes.
>*truly looking*
truly talking
truly touching.

>*Returning to the nectar*
getting love.
giving love.

Fluttering together in figure-8's
Singing the heart's song.
Soaring and gliding
on love's thermals.

Sanctuary
October 9, 1998

On a fall morning I walk in sunshine, mindful of the moment, and know, that wherever I've been going, here I now am. I see my own shadow, blonde-silver hair bouncing before me as I stride along, straight and tall and vibrant, the woman, molded from desert soil, returned.

I wake to soft fresh air and sunlight, streaming into your black hair. With myopic, close-up vision, each strand magnifies into infinite, circular prisms, cathedral rose windows woven together in violet, aqua, indigo and golden strands.

I know you this close. Know you as the jewel of my soul. You, who knows my heart, my breath and my thoughts. You, too, entranced by the desert, taken in like a sailor to the sirens' song.

So, together, we begin anew, in this land of simplicity, serenity and exquisite beauties. This time your touch with humanity shows me the people, as I have never known them before. Like a dense forest of Joshua trees, rooted in the perfect formula of soil, altitude and moisture that ensures survival, this colony of desert dwellers has found community, sense of place, belonging.

I return in humility, and pride. Honoring those who have stayed on, yet possessive of the place as my own. What may I be able to share of myself? Will I truly belong? Will my mother's community become my own? Questions and consciousness confirming that, what the Indians know to be true, is so.

*"The power of the world
works in circles,
and everything tries to be round—
the sky, round, and I have heard that
the earth is round,
making a ball,
and so are all the stars.
The wind, in its greatest power
whirls.
Birds make their nests
in circles,
for theirs is the same
religion as ours.
The sun comes forth
and goes down in a circle,
the moon does the same,
and both are round.
Even the seasons
form a great circle
in their changing,
and always come back again,
to where they were..."*

—Black Elk, 1932

In late fall, 1999, I take a farewell walk in the oak landscape that I have come to know so well these two decades of life in the Santa Ynez Valley. I walk, I sit, I observe. The warm winds out of the southwest brush the dry grassy slopes with alternating soft currents and gusts of force. Leaves of gold and paling green glisten in the sunshine, then sweep across my path as the wind whirls, the dark limbs of the Valley oak baring themselves with each breath of autumn wind, transforming into black silhouettes against a bright blue sky.

I breathe in the pulse of the land, sloping in curvaceousness, rounded and creased with deep canyons and creek beds that beckon to be explored. In a stream of consciousness a databank of acquired vocabulary springs forth: Oak habitat, conservation easements, P&D, urban boundaries, environmental impact, mitigation, private property rights, cluster development, General Plan Update, antiquated parcels, COLAB, consensual approach, sprawl, zoning ordinance, ag viability, agribusiness, CEQA, hidden agenda, watershed management plan, Williamson Act, State Water Project, sustainability, organic produce, joint powers authority, transfer development credits, vineyard management, open space, quality of life. A bantering about in my head of the issues I have delved into as editor of an environmental awareness newsletter.

And with all of this knowledge, I know what is important to me. Sit with someone you love under the night sky. Take a friend into the surrounding hills and hike and touch the earth. Share your simple love of the natural world with a child. Be still in a sacred place that brings you peace and restores your spirit. Pursue your dreams.

So now the circle of life leads me back to the desert, a landscape more familiar and intrinsic than these oak woodlands, a circle that binds Lloyd and me together in a communion of love and commitment, with a shared reverence for the earth and sky that embraces us.

Like our own hearts aching to be revealed, the desert lies waiting, luring us, like prospectors to gold, with treasures we were seeking—simplicity, awareness, appreciation, freedom and partnership. Lloyd and I became pilgrims, entranced by the openness, the 360 degrees of panoramas, the yodel of the coyote chorus, the magical beauty of desert nights, as we camped under the silhouette of Indian Head above town.

But the welcoming acceptance and generous spirit of the folks we met clinched it for us. We came home.

We find a little house in the rocks, and settle into the solid fifty year-old desert home that sits snugly on the land, hugged by acres of undisturbed growth of creosote, yucca, ocotillo, desert willow, cholla, and our own botanical garden of beavertail cactus, with the Joshua Tree National Park boundary to the south and panoramic views of city lights and rock-strewn canyons to the east. Voices of the coyote, quail, wrens and dove tickle the ears, while jack rabbits, kangaroo rats, roadrunners, tortoise and big white lizards entertain us with their antics. A dream come true, for me, to live surrounded by native vegetation and to share the glory of the desert sunrise and sunset with a soulmate!

Solitary Walk
May 31, 2000

This morning the open desert beckons. A moment of solitude begs for the unmarked path, a meandering of mood and spirit to be directed by the flow of the land. So, rather than the pavement of the canyon road and the discipline of an uphill jog around the 49 Palms Canyon loop and back again, today I choose the magnificent wash to the west and surrender to reverie and observation.

The deep sandy road disappears behind me, as I wend my way past the old Dr. Luckie homestead nestled into the rise overlooking the deep wash that leads to Indian Cove. I decide to walk up the ridgeline, hypnotized by the dark rust of the rocks, etched with nature's own petroglyphs forged by wind and water over an unimaginable stretch of geological time. Lines of gray reveal wrinkled facial sculptures. In the brilliance of intensifying sunshine, I sense the rock returning to a molten state, fluid and intensely hot. In the cool of shadows the rocks solidify again, light tan strokes from an ancient paintbrush breaking up the deep rusts and browns of the rocky faces.

Walking the ridges the vegetation of the wash—catsclaw, willow, smoke tree and dry perennial grasses—yields to bleached sand dotted with dark stones. I weave through colonies of pencil cholla and clustered families of yucca, eyes watchful of the shady places where creatures hide. Lizard, cottontail, jackrabbit and quail explode from nowhere when startled. Giant white lizards with large wise eyes startle me!

The mid-morning sun sketches a shadowed statue of liberty torch in the sand, the silhouette of an 8-foot high yucca with baubles of seed pouches around her neck, as spring flowers fade. The dazzling colors of the desert leap out unexpectedly, demanding to be noticed. Clumps of brilliant red mistletoe berries, resembling translucent fish eggs, cling to branches of mesquite. The delicacy of pink crepe paper blossoms on ears of humble beavertail cactus offers a sensuous treat to the eye. The skinny spines of the pencil cholla are a luscious untouchable mix of chartreuse and plum.

    I stoop to run my finger through a black swirl of iron dust in the white sandy wash and wish for a magnet on a string to drag like I did as a child, collecting fuzzy filaments to rub between fingers and collect again.

    This morning I celebrate my homecoming, returning to this landscape of my childhood, and find the girl whose eyes soften into easy wells of memory, forever touched by simplicity of word, touch, and the startling beauty of the natural world that rekindles faith in the divine without sermon or dogma.

    A familiar sense of solitude, within myself, continues to give me strength, to feed my soul. That quiet spot that is my center, that space of wonderment, still the same, yet deeper, fuller, shared now with one who knows. Today I walk without the restlessness of youth; no hollow space of longing, but a stillness of spirit grounded in self-acceptance and a shared knowledge of the profound power of faith, honesty and tenacity.

    Gladness and sadness, fulfillment and desire, contentment and aspiration, all a rich oneness, the paradox that makes my life swell with meaning.

    I belong here, in this desertscape, as never before. No time of adjustment, no letting go of the past to embrace the present, just the present in all its beauty, and all that each moment offers for discovery—of place, of self, of community. The blending of the past into what is present and the endless becoming into future.

    I follow the ridge all the way up to the edge of the Indian Cove wash, where the mesquite grows dense and deep green, but up close is covered with miniature baby yellow cotton candy blossoms abuzz with wild bee song. The tumble of rocks curves into the embracing heights of Indian Cove. I am tempted to walk all the way to the campgrounds, but the sun is high above and I must turn back now.

    I take the low sweep of the sandy wash for my homeward path. No other footprints but mine are visible, just the deep imprints of an old horse trail, and silently I say thank-you to the National Park System and to all those vigilant folks who rallied for desert preservation, for acquiring this section of the land just for me, for this special day of solitary wanderings and wonder, in my new home, the desert of my youth.

Reflections

...a July evening

Sunset. Cloudy. Swaths of brilliant peach and pink, swirling in ever-changing textures and waves. A pressure change pulls in moisture from the southwest and a refreshing breeze calls me outside, as the clouds move across the sun, providing welcome relief from a dogged sun that has kept the temperatures high, 108 and upward.

I must walk in the wind. The gathering clouds and the colors of twilight have me singing inwardly, a Hallelujah chorus, in praise of this moment of sensitivity, the feel of wind in my hair, breathing this fresh air, savoring the wide expansiveness of the desert around me.

This freedom to roam is my Mass, my prayerfulness, my Communion. It is pure beauty, and it fills my soul.

...an early September morning

Giant tortoise sighting. Big armored tank roaring through our backyard at .005 miles per hour, heading NNE. Last seen venturing toward the driveway.

An armada of quail emerge from the desert floor, clucking and squawking. Eight of them crowd onto the bird feeder, seed flying. Sixteen others peck the ground.

Now the dove arrive. One innocent, lovely one, soon joined by her doting partner. They appear timid in the presence of the plump, domineering quail.

Morning entertainment.

...welcome fall

The wind is gusting and the temperature drops, the first day of autumn is here. Lloyd has a fever and flu and has gone to bed after a supper of chicken soup and tea.

Benny Goodman plays on, that joyful nostalgic music of the '40s that makes you want to dance to the familiar rhythms heard in childhood. I can feel my feet flicking over the floor, my skirt swaying!

The wind continues to blast. I sit and enjoy the textures of our desert home—the round woven baskets over the front window, the yellows, blues and greens in the rug, a collection of glassware, vases, copper candlesticks, odds and ends of collected pottery on the mantle; the leafiness of the tall ficus tree I have nurtured now for over 20 years; the wicker arm chair we bought for our birthday; Lloyd's mother's antique black birdcage hung from the ceiling, with the wooden hummingbird my son bought me hovering inside. Such a pleasing tapestry we have woven together, of our pasts and our mutual present.

The music is off. Only the wind provides a tune, galloping wildly, then pausing momentarily, then blasting. A fluid wave of sound—the wind rushing in water-like currents. I hear and feel it, swirling, wrapping around the corners of the house, then rushing out into open spaces. Out and away. More waves rolling in, roaring, gushing to the canyons and valley below.

Last Monday we camped at Cottonwood, packing our VW bus with pillows, blankets, candles, BBQ supplies, soap and towels. Through the ocotillo patch we drove in the Pinto Basin, stopping to marvel at their leafiness, so green and lush a forest after late summer rains.

We found a private space, only two other campers in the whole campground. The rains have flooded the campsite. No footprints but our own. We cooked pork chops and sliced potatoes and onions on the grill, drank wine and melted under the immensity of dark space and the wide dusty blanket of the Milky Way. Up and out we looked for what seemed like hours, lost in the vastness of our universe. Satisfied. Together. Still. Reverent.

...a late afternoon in September

It is so beautiful, it hurts. How can that be? Be it yet so true? The light sharpens focus, an autumn phenomenon. Precisely yesterday fall arrived. Sound carries differently today. Stillness reigns. Yellows dominate the palette, carpeting the sand, sprinkled in blossoms on the new green of creosote, on the golden spines of the pencil cholla.

The rocks, large and shiny, are outlined with shimmering sunlight. And the greens, sage, pea green, emerald, all reaching skyward in a choreography of verdant growth.

Bumble bees, black and buzzing, hummingbirds and grey sparrows with black capes and chests, beauty all around me.

This morning an awesome new visitor graced our breakfast window, a giant golden hawk, larger than imaginable when seen up so close. Flying in, then away, out of sight, hopefully to return again.

I sit outside our bedroom window in my beach chair, the tops of my feet burning in the last rays of sunlight. One lone morning glory blossom shrivels in the late afternoon, but an unopened bud, two leaves down, promises to brighten our day tomorrow morning. Each vein with the sunny backdrop behind the leaves is outlined in precise pathways. Next fall I will plant morning glory seeds to honor this one plant sprouted from Solvang soil.

...unexpected company

Two wrens came for a visit this afternoon. Flying in through the top half of the Dutch door, while I hung laundry on the line out back. They banged frantically against the window panes above the desk, then against the kitchen window. I closed the blinds above the table and they then saw their escape through the open door.

Beautiful speckled wings and a bratty voice, the cactus wrens. My favorite desert bird. They construct intriguing nests in the pencil cholla, strung together with old Lipton tea bags and tags, scraps of fabric, feathers from fellow birds, sticks, strands of hair—all woven together in a marvelous tapestry wedged cleverly among sharp, uninviting cactus spines.

Freedom Ride

After an easy-going September morning of puttering, I kidnap Lloyd and head out east of town on Hwy. 62. I have packed our VW camper with roasted vegetables, baked potatoes and lamb chops to BBQ, just in case the trek turns into an overnighter. I turn off on Gold Crown Road and trade places with Lloyd to let him drive. We are going to explore the Old Dale Mining District!

The road beckons gently enough as we head out across rocky soil that is firm and drivable with ease. A woman Park Ranger in a 4-wheel drive Toyota meets us head on and advises us not to proceed, as the road ahead alternates with very deep soft sand and an impassable rocky road, which tends to slip out from under her in spots.

Undeterred, we venture on, crossing the first of many washes of soft deep sand. "Keep moving!" I squeal as we forge ahead. Some days are just ripe for adventure and the thrill of an untraveled road with scenery like this, why would it ever enter into your head to turn back, when each curve offers a new landscape, another sweeping vista and yet another specimen of unusual desert plant life to get out and examine up close?

Stopping at a steep overlook, Lloyd gets out and hollers into the vast open desert below, "Whardahfahgahwee?" One of his unique expressions of tribal identity.

The transition zone between the Mojave and the Colorado deserts proves the most challenging. We drag our skid plate over rocks and ravines, high-centering and spinning our wheels for a rollicking good ride, collecting a sampling of souvenir stones in our bumper as we slip and slide along, our laughter and my howls of unfettered delight ricocheting off the blackened rocks of surrounding downward-sloping canyons.

I egg my *Pinto Man* onward and onward, as our journey leads south onto the expansive floor of the Pinto Basin, past remnants of the old mining era, rusty corrugated tin water troughs, slabs of rough old concrete and unusual objects that could be an ore smelter, a crematoria or perhaps a bread oven. Wooden signs marking the Brooklyn Mine Trail and the intersection of Black Eagle Mine Road promise the lure of future roads to roam.

    Incredible blue skies and endless horizons guide us to the refuge of a camping spot at Jumbo Rocks, offering an evening of dining and snuggling under the stars and a morning awakening surrounded by a myriad of suggestive boulder shapes, whose shades of peach, tans and flesh tones lure you in like sirens, enticing you to strip down to your own bare shape to blend into the pallet of rounded granite rocks.

    The freedom and joy of this adventure live on as the measure of how carefree and intimate our desert days were. For the rest of my days I will continually circle back to the cherished memory of this spontaneous trek across my beloved desert with my forever moon-man.

Yuletide, 2001

In the night the north wind asserts his power over the sun, buffeting against the block walls of our little home in the rocks, wailing around the corners with a crescendo of whistles in the pine needles of the big tree out back, as we hunker down deeper into our blankets; then trumpeting down through the canyons releasing its force into the valley below.

Today the icy hand of winter massages the skies with a blanket of fast-moving clouds, iced with lacy white frosting against a backdrop of brilliant cornflower blue.

The flesh tones of boulder and stone stand firm, yet yielding gracefully, patiently, grain-by-grain, to the forces of geologic time.

Through the v-cut in the ridgeline my eyes scan the northeastern skyline, where the powdery dust of tanks preparing for war floats eerily behind the Bullion Mountains.

Over the decades of space and time, Einstein's thoughts ride the currents of the wind—close encounters with the divine, face-to-face, intellect-to-intellect—revealing that "you cannot simultaneously prevent and prepare for war."

The tank tracks continue to riddle the soft sands, the boom of cannons a battle-of-the-bands with the north wind.

The true test lies when the dust settles and we stand eye-to-eye with the aged child-soldier. How to decode the warrior mind? How to embrace him with tenderness, peace and the brotherhood of humanity, when the only arms he has known for all his years is the steel barrel of the rifle in his hand?

I turn back to the steadfast embrace of stones. Heaps of boulders, an ancient altar of patience, peace, balance and serenity.

> Winds of winter, flaming the creative.
> Breath, an ode to stillness of spirit.
> Peace on earth.
> Man-to-man.

*The moon persists in casting her moody glow
through drifting layers of cloud cover.
Even to the far west her scattered rays of dim light
paint a soft cottony glow
beneath the pressing moisture of deep grey.*

*My mood follows the lunar path—
begging to be seen and recognized,
and even adored—
then slipping behind a dense shroud,
wanting anonymity and privacy—
even wanting to be left alone,
perhaps,
invisible,
behind the layers of deep grey.*

*Soft, swirling.
A subtle halo giving away
the lunar presence...*

Heat Waves

I wake to the jolt of sunrise,
red-orange blossoms swaying
in the gentle breeze of dawn,
sky an unfiltered perfect blue.
Behind my eyelids—
images of pen-and-ink figures,
woman-shapes,
washed in bright watercolors,
the feminine contours formed by
names of flowers and herbs.
Botanical names in indigo blue,
crimson and gold,
bold writings embracing the figures
in emerald greens and scarlet, violet,
and black ink.
Desert birds of paradise.

Now the gentle morning breeze
bathes the fire in me,
this heat flowing from the core—
chest, neck and back of arms,
this inner fire,
embers,
hot,
escaping in tides of flashing warmth.
New tides.
Not the soft tidal waves of moonbeams,
but a new red tide of heat,
seeking an escape hatch,
through my pores.
This is where I am,
in this new chapter of my days.

These heat waves speak of passions,
perhaps,
new creative forces boiling in me,
seeking expression.
There is sunshine in my soul, after-all.
How to voice this new heat?
Let it brew,
to speak for itself.
Listen, and stay open
to what heat means.
This sunshine on my shoulders,
behind my breastbone,
bolting like lightening flashes,
jarring me to wakefulness.
Let me be awake!

The brush fire brings
new growth,
succulent, springtime green,
delicate flowers
in the ashes.
"Let the fire fall!"

Champion of the Creosote

Not surprisingly, my passion led me to become an activist for the protection of my beloved native vegetation from the indiscriminate grading that I was witnessing on parcels under development. I became the champion of the creosote.

So horrified was I, that I gathered up fellow citizens, Lloyd and I and others collecting a volume of signatures, to create a voice larger than my own for the formation of an ordinance to uphold the existing wording in the City's General Plan. This wording spoke to the limiting of grading on parcels one acre or larger, but lacked the teeth for enforcement.

I was appointed by the Planning Commission to chair an Ad Hoc Citizens Committee. For a year, members of the Morongo Basin Conservation Association joined with me and together we plugged along within the system working on the draft of a grading ordinance to prevent the impacts of erosion and air quality degradation that results from clear cutting of native vegetation.

The intent spoke to the City's century-old heritage of homesteading, which persists today, as people continue to seek out the healthy climate, natural beauty and lifestyle that the unique high desert environment offers.

The meetings were stimulating, hopeful and taxing. But, when it came time to go forward, the City fathers balked. One Councilman openly questioned whether this ordinance "would keep him from developing his 25 acres the way he intended."

In the end, the wording was watered down into a statement inserted into the Development Code, but the efforts for an ordinance were not satisfied.

As a result, in the following "boom-and-bust" years of the decade, hundreds of acres have been desecrated by the standard practice of developers, who lack the vision that personal spirit of place embodies. A rectangular grid is placed over the contours of the desert, all vegetation is removed, and the fragile desert soils are consequentially destabilized, leaving us with no recourse.

I wanted to make a difference. I put all my energies into it, even though my temperament is not compatible with the constant state of doing battle and being on the defensive, that working in an entrenched system demands. Consensus building appears to be something that we American people are still learning, and that is even perceived by some as a threat to the individual rights of our American experience.

A uniform standard for developers was not pursued at that time. However, ten years later, another citizen committee is working once again on this same issue, hopefully with better results than our initial effort. Perhaps the groundwork we laid will make their path less formidable.

Backroads VW

"Just what is it you do here?" a friend from the Historical Society wondered out loud, as he came in the front door.

"You just walked through it!" we laughed from our chairs in the office of our VW parts shop, where a couple of folks were relaxing and chatting around our desk.

"Backroads VW" was the business we had opened in our newly purchased building on Adobe Road next to the Fire Station. Lloyd had a large selection of air-cooled VW parts for early Bugs and transporters, so, we mused, why not open a shop and sell the inventory from his 35-plus years of mechanic-ing?

The block building sat on two lots and was originally the town barbershop in the early '30s. We spruced up the walls with sage green paint and built shelving units to organize the electrical, brake and engine parts, hanging accelerator and brake cables on pegboards and purchasing a few chrome pieces to attract the Baja Bug and dune buggy folks.

And what folks they were! Lloyd welcomed humanity in without judgment, quick to spot trouble and open to listening to the sincere, young and old.

We met an array of individuals—school teachers, young gung-ho Marines training for Operation Desert Storm, teenagers with heavy duty bolts plugged into their earlobes (Ubangi Joe and Zulu, Lloyd nicknamed them) hippie-era women with unusual colorful names and even more peculiar behavior, senior citizens towing a mini-trailer behind their bright yellow Bug, a Vietnam vet suffering from Agent Orange-related disabilities, and even a meth addict who vehemently threw his parts back at me when they weren't what he wanted.

With fellow VW enthusiasts, we helped form the High Desert VW Classics Club, showcasing the first-ever line-up of vintage Volkswagens in the annual Pioneer Days Parade.

The high point of our Backroads VW connections was befriending Ralph, a German customer who proved to be one of the wisest, most intelligent beings on the planet. A master machinist, he loved testing Lloyd's knowledge about engine building or axles. He and Lloyd would stand together at the counter drawing detailed pictures to explain the pros and cons of different applications and peculiarities of the People's Car.

Ralph lived a few miles east of town in an unfinished house he called "The Ruins." On the top of his '68 Bug he'd built a metal frame for his mattress for solitary ventures way out into the desert for nights of star-gazing and exploring. He devised a unique pry bar tool to use when he would get stuck in deep sand during his solitary explorations out into the desert.

One cold, rainy Saturday afternoon Ralph's car broke down in the bank parking lot in Yucca Valley. Not knowing anyone else who could rescue him, he phoned Lloyd, who, of course, was willing to help out. He hooked the VW up to a tow bar, and with Ralph preferring to stay at the wheel inside his own car, we pulled him home behind us. He insisted on giving us his groceries in gratitude.

Ralph shared his inventions and his philosophies openly with us, a gentle soul, who believed that the energy of good balances out the evil, and what you put out into the universe returns likewise onto you.

There were long, hot summer afternoons I sprawled across a couple of VW seats and fell asleep in a pool of sweat, while Lloyd languished in the heat with his head on the counter. Some days no one came in. We folded a dollar bill in half and framed it with our City Business License to commemorate our first sale of 50 cents.

There was ample time to daydream. Cleaning the yard, pulling the sand and windblown trash through the tines of my rake, I developed "business plans" of my own design. For my "Bus Stop" idea we acquired half a dozen VW campers to tuck into special nooks in the desert landscape on the pristine acreage near the Park entrance that I had scrounged to purchase for this venture. I made a logo design with a VW camper under a water tank tower and drew concepts for a storage shed and a chuck wagon circle for BBQing and storytelling under the stars. Tourists could rent a VW bus to camp in on long weekends, under the gaze of the Indian Head rock outcropping to the west.

"The Volksgallerie" could be set up where our office was. An exhibit of nature-inspired artwork of every medium, watercolors and oils, photography, jewelry, sculpture. My daughter suggested a Kaffee Haus, since we spent so much time gabbing and giving directions to people who wandered in. Mom thought a "Weinstube" would be perfect, given my recent stint in the Firestone Vineyard's tasting room. Or how about an outdoor theater on Friday nights with classic movies, popcorn and sodas as a fundraiser for the Historical Society?

Many who came in asked us to make keys, assuming we were still the former key shop owners. Most came in just to talk or pass the time of day. Others dredged knowledge and expertise from Lloyd's wealth of experience, only to order their parts in the new way, "on-line," or from a discount catalog. A lot requested Lloyd to work on their cars, but we were not licensed to do so, and could only provide verbal help, as tempting as it was for Lloyd to just gather up his tools and set up a mechanics shop once again.

Lloyd started coming in early to putter on our own cars under the shade of the fruitless mulberry tree out back. His presence lured in more customers and soon we were meeting our goal of making enough to pay our monthly mortgage on the building. How proud and satisfied we were with our humble progress.

And then Tom died. My husband's son. The ensuing whirlpool cast us into an eddy of spiraling responsibilities. Back and forth between the desert and the coast we boomeranged. Our sweet desert interlude was to be short-lived, as, consequently, back to the Santa Ynez Valley we were called, to oversee the commercial property, where Tiffany's Auto Repair had flourished for over 25 years, back where our love story had begun, in the garage.

A man's identity is forged by the tools he's held in his hands, from the moment he first gripped a wrench to help his mother start her gas-powered wringer washing machine, mixing the gas and oil in proper proportions; or when his father entrusted him with a hatchet and took his young son along with him into the Wisconsin woods, where the child stripped bark from the railroad ties at his Uncle's lumber mill; later the adolescent walking barefoot into the classroom with wrenches in his back pocket and grease on his jeans.

Sure and steadfast, his skill and forthright honesty became acknowledged and appreciated by the wealth of friendship and goodwill that surrounded him. Work and the man, one. The tools of a mechanic, a bond strong and essential to spirit.

She is nourished by the wide-open spaces, by the sure rotation of the constellations that sweep across immense black skyscape, the sun's greeting at dawn, the breath of soft air that stirs the curtain and causes her to rouse.

She walks freely, without confinement, to the overlook at the wash to watch the sun set, turning pink and bronze, casting late afternoon shadows that transform grays to purples and grey-green to chartreuse.

She strides across the desert with the coyote couple paralleling her path, disappearing like ghosts into the scrub, blending into the landscape of yucca, creosote and saltbush.

A desert moonchild.

Dreams and the Bighorn

The woman-child holds on to her dreams.
And her memories.
Past, present and future
blending into one another,
like molten rock.
Journal entries, calendar pages,
visions and fantasies —
layers of geological schist.

A child's game of hopscotch etched in the desert sand.
Surface waters rippling.
Sun shining on muscled shoulders,
kayak paddles blading through the current.
Bonfires and campouts.
Sweet lovemaking
and walks on endless beaches.
Souls touching souls,
uniting in the moment's meteor shower.
Hiking the slick rock.
Dancing with hot Mojave thermals
on the wings of a magical white-winged bird.
Witnessing a newborn's face,
awestruck and open,
to all possibilities of this new world.

Real and unreal.
Imagination knowing no boundaries
of time or space,
only the possible —
of what was, what is,
and what can be.

She lived on the edge of wild,
yet sometimes felt the wild eluding her.
She knew she must walk out —
into the canyon where no other footsteps trod.
Leaving telephone poles, horse trails and barbed wire fence,
any sign of the built environment behind,
she walked.

Up the wash,
swirled with the paw print of wild ones.
Scrapings and scuffing in the sands of the wash,
unfamiliar.
The canyon lured her on,
a rocky, seemingly dead-end ravine.
Something made her stop.
Something peripheral. Blurred movement.
Startled, yet no remembrance of sound.

Then, breathless, she saw them.

Them!
Count them.
1.2.3.4.5.
No, 6.
Bighorn sheep.
Moving up the facing slope,
grazing on native bunch grass.
Watching her.

Tears came to her eyes.
She knelt in the wash,
in the blind of creosote,
and cried.
"Mystical," the word whispered, within.
"In the awesome presence
of the bighorn."

They continue to graze.
Only the big ram,
with his radiant curl of horns,
is disturbed.
He paws the ground.
The rest of the herd moves slowly,
up higher onto the rocky slope.
One, particularly white and roan-colored,
lingers in the shade,
near the ram.

She feels like an invader,
of their privacy,
of their territory.
The ram turns and faces her.
Direct.
She feels threatened,
even though she knows better.
He is 100 yards away,
yet still he seems to challenge her.
He moves forward,
in her direction.
She retreats down the wash.
Then returns to perch on an opposite rocky slope to watch.
1.2.3.4.5.
Where is he?
6.
Stillness.
Yet all the rocks around her seem to move.
Fluid, ghostlike.
Alive? Or just stone?
She strains her eyes for a glimpse of them.
They have moved almost to the top of the ridge.
Rocks or rams?
No binoculars to bring them into sharper focus.
1.2.3.
Is that him watching her, face on, or,
Illusion?

Whatever thoughts prevailed
when she first stepped into the wild
have now disseminated with the breeze.
"There is only this rugged canyon,
these yucca, boulders,
and our breath.
As we watch one another."
1.2. on the rocky horizon to the south.
Stones tumble.
"I hear you."
More rocks tumble.
Loud.
Like gunshots in absolute stillness,

of desert sky and winter sunshine.
Not rocks tumbling,
but horns crashing against horns.
One sheep leaps backwards,
a silhouette on the ridgeline.
Then disappears.
Silence.
Still the ram watches her,
from the center of the slope,
sunlight bouncing off his hide.
How much time does one have?
The wild know no time.

Coyotes howl from the wash to the west.
Again. More this time.
Their yodeling echoes off the rocks.
The air is chilled now.
Late afternoon sunshine turns creosote to a rusty glow,
ignites the grasses on the slopes into miniature golden torches.
Dried yucca flowers glisten like crowns.
Ravens caw.
Still the ram holds his ground, mid-slope.
Ever alert.

She turns to go,
several times glancing back,
for a final glimpse of him.
He stands motionless,
holding her firm in his line of sight,
sun bouncing off his curled horns.
A sculpture,
unmoving,
in a frozen moment of grace.

The land slants northward,
and she follows the curve of the earth
to return home.
The woman-child,
forever in a state of becoming,
dreams and memories
held firmly in her heart.

Afterword

"The Unfinished Fence"

Once upon a time, Dad started building a fence around the north and west side of the house. Fence posts were laboriously sunk into the ground, leveled and cemented in. But only across the front did the actual boards get nailed up to screen the yard, where the septic tank was known to overflow periodically into embarrassing cesspoolish situations.

Dad never quite got around to putting up the boards along the western property line, and, before long, the unfinished fence became a metaphor for living. "When are you going to finish the fence?" was a good question to ask if you wanted evasive answers.

When you're dealing with an unfinished project, you're always working creatively on it in your head. It subliminally occupies your thought waves, so you can never be accused of hosting a devil's workshop in your idle mind.

And, you're also sort of stuck. Can't start a new endeavor. No way to justify another project when you've got this other one hanging out there unfinished, yet brewing with such potential.

Like this particular piece of writing, which I started some years ago, "Growing Up Desert." I've shared excerpts of it with family members and so it's become publicly known that I am working on a personal writing project. I've even given readings at coffee houses and at a mural dedication in the very hometown that spawned the entire writings. Perhaps I thought by stating it out loud I could actually make it happen and ward off other involvements.

But, there it stands, like the unfinished fence. "How's the writing coming?" friends and family ask. "Well, life happens. Gets in the way." I josh. Is that such a good rationale, when doodads are keeping me from finishing this personally important work that I began with such focus and passion?

For an artist the finished product never measures up to the original vision of the creation anyway. Better to hold the "perfect" version in your mind's eye than to present an imperfect finished product to the rest of the world! Packaged in a semi-finished mode, I wonder if that's diminished my need to finish this writing project. It's already mentally finished. I know the ending. Or, I thought I did, when I wrote all the notes down a long time ago, while I sat in the pits at one of my son's motocross races!

And, really, is there a known ending? Life goes on! Who needs the whole yard fenced anyway? The unfinished fence keeps you there. Keeps you from resolving old dilemmas and moving on. Keeps you in the process of developing your sense of place till you just can't leave the place.

That unfinished fence with just a few finished boards, all painted up and pretty, kept Dad in his desert home and has kept this child of his rooted deeply in the shiftless sands of a brilliant masterpiece begging to be completed!

Perhaps the story has no ending or embraces more than one completed piece of work. There is the blessing of this present moment, the gift of yet another day, with all its riches. At any rate, there is not just one circle, but many interwoven concentric circles. And the circles, round and round, always lead homeward.

"...We can live happily elsewhere for awhile, but the time will come when one of us goes starry eyed and sooner or later the same terse comment will be uttered: I have to get back to the desert and that is all."

—Elizabeth Crozier Campbell
"The Desert Was Home"

In Memoriam

Mom's Eulogy, Blessed Sacrament School
January 14, 2016

When Lloyd and I first started coming out to 29 together, we found the desert just kept luring us back time and again. So we bought a little fixer-upper as a sanctuary for our more and more frequent visits.

The closing of Escrow happened to coincide with the dedication of the Flash Flood Mural, so I phoned our Realtor, now our very dear friend, Larry Briggs, and I asked him if he knew who was in charge of the dedication ceremony.

"Well, it so happens I am," he said.

So I told him I had this bit of writing I'd done about growing up on the desert, and how as kids we played in the flood waters, and I thought it might be appropriate for the dedication of this mural, and that I'd like to surprise my mother by reading it at the ceremony.

He hesitated for a moment, probably thinking this was a bit presumptuous of a newcomer from the Santa Ynez Valley.

"Well, who's your mother?" he asked.

"Margot Spangenberg."

"Oh, my gosh! Margot!" he exclaimed. "You're on!"

And that was my official reintroduction to my hometown.

Once Lloyd and I started living in 29 fulltime, it didn't take many introductions to realize that being Margot's daughter was the "Open Sesame" to acceptance and inclusion. All of us Spangenberg children owe so much to Mom, to her devotion to this community, her profound spirit of place. She made 29 Palms her own, and you all made her yours.

How she loved us all.

About the Author

Chris Tiffany moved from San Pedro, California, where she was born, to the High Desert community of 29 Palms in 1953. The Oasis of Mara, at the northern entrance to Joshua Tree National Park, was her childhood playground.

Since age 10 she has kept personal diaries and journals and credits her writing talent to her mother, Margot Spangenberg.

A graduate of University of California, Irvine, Tiffany is a former director of the Santa Ynez Valley Family School, whose curriculum encourages exploration of the surrounding Los Padres National Forest as an extension of the classroom.

A 40-year resident of the Santa Ynez Valley, she is a past editor of the Women's Environmental Watch newsletter. For many years she served as the initial publicist and program coordinator for Arts Outreach, the local community arts organization.

She continues to enjoy frequent retreats to her cabin on the boundary of Joshua Tree National Park.

www.ingramcontent.com/pod-product-compliance
Lightning Source LLC
Chambersburg PA
CBHW072006290426
44109CB00018B/2154